KITCHEN HERO
GREAT FOOD FOR LESS

DONAL SKEHAN

KITCHEN HERO
GREAT FOOD FOR LESS

DONAL SKEHAN

Collins

CONTENTS

INTRODUCTION

This book is quite simply about the tricks of thrifty cooking and cheap eating. For my generation in particular, who have grown up in a time where pre-washed salad bags, ready-grated cheese and plastic-wrapped convenience foods have become everyday purchases, thrifty cooking practices can seem like they are from a forgotten world. However, any good cook will know that these are skills that have been used for years, to save money and eat better food. Now is the time to rediscover these great cooking traditions and stop relying on convenience foods, which cost us more and are of inferior quality to dishes that can be made at home. Banish any thoughts of penny-pinching: this is about embracing home cooking at its very best. The real aim here is to make inexpensive ingredients work harder for the money you spend on them, so that ultimately you end up with delicious food that will become part of your everyday diet.

My grandmother is one of the most frugal self-taught cooks you will ever meet: she raised my mom and her six siblings with very little income, but that never stopped her producing wonderfully elegant meals at minimum expense. Her long-engrained home-cooking skills, using inexpensive materials and simple methods, are some of the greatest kitchen tips that have been passed on to me. There is a whole army of grandparents, parents, aunts and uncles up and down the country who possess and use these skills without giving them a second thought. Many of them may have been brought up in households with tight budgets, where watching the pennies was part and parcel of daily life. Some of my favourite recipes and cooking practices in this book are ones I've learnt as a result of just chatting on the topic of frugal cooking with those in the know – from my own family to butchers, greengrocers and fishmongers.

This book begins with my frugal cooking guide, in which I've included some of the top economical tips and tricks that have been passed on to me: from ways to make your cooking easier and more efficient to general practices that will save you money. There are one or two recipes in the book that will be more expensive to make than others, but the important thing to remember is that these will usually feed a crowd or leave you with leftovers that will keep you going for a few days. My dessert and baking recipes are a good reminder that frugal cooking doesn't have to mean missing out.

The chapters in this book are filled with recipes that I hope will become part of your cooking routine. They are all simple to follow and don't require any complicated kitchen equipment, so even those with very few cooking skills can be encouraged to try their hand at them. For those who love to cook on a regular basis, I'd encourage you to try using old-fashioned ingredients, such as offal, or underused cuts of meat. I hope all the recipes will inspire you to try a new approach to cooking – one that is hugely satisfying for your appetite as well as your wallet.

COOKING
ON A SHOESTRING

a frugal cooking guide

Cooking frugally is all about what I call 'clever cooking', and by that I mean using what you have, saving leftovers to use again, make-ahead preparation, utilising your freezer and choosing inexpensive ingredients that will go far. An understanding of the skills employed by butchers and fishmongers will help you to choose the best ingredients for cheaper prices, so in this section I've outlined the main things you should consider when cooking with meat and fish, as well as advice on other ingredients.

Understanding the seasonality of food is an important part of clever cooking: for example, buying out-of-season strawberries or asparagus in December will not only cost you more but you will most likely have a lesser-quality, tasteless ingredient that has been flown halfway across the world – not good for the environment or for your cooking. In recent years, growing your own vegetables has also become a popular way to help save money and encourage awareness of seasonality – you need very little space, a few containers, a bag or two of soil and some seeds to produce ingredients that can otherwise cause a dent in your weekly shopping bill.

A quick word about organic produce: when and if you can afford it, do try to choose organic. Organic fruit and vegetables are not sprayed with pesticides, and organic meat is free of antibiotics and the animals will have been ethically reared and slaughtered. Always try to choose free-range poultry and eggs. It is more expensive, but there is, of course, a price to be paid for the quality of the food we choose to eat.

BUTCHER

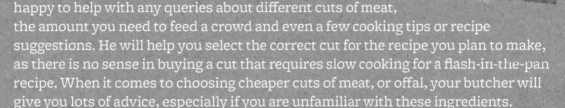

It's important to support your local butcher as much as possible. The skills of a good butcher are essential ones to harness as a home cook. Your butcher will be happy to help with any queries about different cuts of meat, the amount you need to feed a crowd and even a few cooking tips or recipe suggestions. He will help you select the correct cut for the recipe you plan to make, as there is no sense in buying a cut that requires slow cooking for a flash-in-the-pan recipe. When it comes to choosing cheaper cuts of meat, or offal, your butcher will give you lots of advice, especially if you are unfamiliar with these ingredients.

Meat can be one of the more expensive ingredients on the weekly shopping bill, so utilising cheaper cuts is the perfect way to reduce costs. However, many cheaper cuts of meat have become unfashionable in modern times, and while they might have made everyday dinners in our grandparents' time, nowadays most people don't know what they are or how to cook them, even though they are still readily available. We are definitely missing a trick, though, because some of the most delicious recipes, such as crispy Asian pork belly, tender oxtail and slowly cooked spiced lamb shoulder, are revelations and prove that these less-expensive cuts really deliver in the flavour department.

People today have a meat-heavy diet, largely due to the fact that meat has become more and more accessible and is conveniently packaged in plastic, meaning that consumers have lost any connection with where the meat actually comes from. Understanding and learning where different cuts of meat originate from on an animal not only helps you to be more economical but it also gives us, as home cooks, a better understanding of the ingredients we are cooking with. In this section I outline some of the cheaper cuts of meats and meat products, many of which are included in recipes throughout this book. Give them a try, and you will be happily surprised by the results!

Finally, while I love my meat, I do think it's important to keep a balance, so try to eat a varied diet and cook some meals that are not completely centred around meat.

PORK

It's important to ask questions about the meat you buy, and this goes for pork in particular. With it being such a regular part of modern everyday diets, corners are often cut in the production of pork products. Ask for meat from pigs that have been reared slowly with natural feed. Good-quality pork meat should have a soft pale-pink colour. The main retail cuts of fresh pork are shoulder, loin, belly and leg. Some cheap cuts to ask for are:

Pork shoulder
The discovery of this cut while writing this book was a real revelation for me. It's incredibly cheap, really delicious and feeds a crowd. Try using it in my Porchetta recipe on page 46. Meat from this cut is quite fatty, so it suits slow roasting at a low temperature for incredibly tender meat, and produces beautifully crispy crackling.

Pork belly
Pork belly is a widely popular cut of meat in Asia, and is loved for its fantastic crispy crackling and tender meat. It's very affordable and easy to cook.

Pork kidneys
Ask your butcher to prepare these for you into nice strips. You should soak the kidneys either in water with lemon juice or in buttermilk for an hour or so, to make the flavour milder and remove any bitterness.

Ham hock
A ham hock is an extremely cheap cured cut of ham from the thigh of the pig. Hocks need to be boiled for an hour or two to make the meat tender, after which the meat can be shredded and used in a huge variety of dishes; it also freezes nicely (see page 42).

Trotters
Also known as crubeens in Ireland, these may not be the most attractive of pork cuts but they are certainly tasty. They are wonderful added to stocks or stews to produce a rich, thick gravy, as they contain quite a lot of gelatin.

Sausage meat
For a cheaper alternative to minced pork, you can buy sausage meat from most butchers. Use it wherever you would minced pork, or add seasonings, wrap in puff pastry and bake in the oven for homemade sausage rolls.

 # BEEF

When buying more expensive cuts of beef, such as fillet or sirloin, make sure to look for meat with a deep, rich, red colour and good marbling (little streaks of fat running through it). These streaks of fat melt away during the cooking process, essentially keeping the meat moist. Try to avoid meat that looks grey, or meat that is a really bright red colour, which can indicate that it hasn't been hung for long enough. With the cheaper cuts of meat, you will find a lot more fat and muscle tissue; these add a richness to the meat when it's cooked slowly over a low heat. Inexpensive cuts to look out for are:

Beef shin
When cooked slowly in the oven, shin of beef becomes meltingly tender and delicious. Use it on the bone; it will enrich any stew or casserole you add it to.

Skirt steak
Skirt steak has a good marbling of fat and is often best used sliced up in stir-fries. However, make sure not to overcook it, as it can become tough.

Chuck steak
Chuck steak is an inexpensive cut from the neck and shoulder of the cow. It can be quite tough, so does not suit fast cooking methods, but it is ideal slowly braised or chopped into pieces and stewed.

Beef brisket
Beef brisket comes from the lower chest of the animal and, like many of the cheaper cuts, is quite tough, so requires slow braising to make it beautifully tender. It is a boneless cut of meat, which makes for easy carving and is perfect for pot-roasts.

Oxtail
Oxtail is perfectly suited for slow braising and stewing and is wonderful for making rich beef stock. When the tough muscle tissue is slowly cooked over a low heat you are left with beautifully tender meat. Try this in my dad's oxtail recipe on page 48!

POULTRY

Mass consumption of chicken has meant it is no longer a special-occasion ingredient but an everyday one. If your budget allows, choose free-range and/or organic chicken, for the health of the birds, ourselves and the environment. When you buy a whole chicken, use all the meat and save the carcass to make stock. If you buy portioned poultry, legs and thighs are cheapest and the most flavourful. Also, don't forget turkey; this underused meat is cheap, but tasty, and turkey mince makes a healthier and cheaper alternative to pork and beef mince.

Basic rich chicken stock

1. Put at least 2–3 roasted chicken carcasses into a large 9-litre (16-pint) pot and fill with cold water to just below the rim.

2. Add about eight black peppercorns, an onion sliced in half (with its skin on), two bay leaves, two peeled carrots and two celery stalks.

3. Bring to the boil, then reduce the heat and simmer gently for 2 hours, skimming any fat or froth from the top every now and then.

4. Strain the stock through a sieve or colander and discard everything but the liquid.

5. The stock can be used in soups, stews, sauces and more. If you want to freeze it, allow to cool before dividing amongst freezer bags and placing in the freezer.

Portioning chicken in 5 easy steps

Buying a whole bird is by far the most economical way to buy chicken, and learning how to portion it into eight pieces is a good practice which allows you to use each part separately as needed.

1. Place the chicken on a chopping board breast-side up and use a sharp knife to slice off the wings, one at a time, by inserting the knife where the wings meet the carcass. You should be able to get the knife into the socket and slice through easily.

2. Pull one of the legs upwards and slice in between the leg and body until you meet resistance at the socket. Slice down through this and remove the leg. Repeat with the second leg.

3. Pull the leg and thigh away from each other and then insert the knife at the join and slice through. Repeat with the other leg.

4. Slice the remaining carcass in half horizontally to remove the backbone, and save this for stock.

5. Flatten the breasts on the board and use the knife to slice down the centre to separate the two halves. You now have eight separate pieces of chicken: two each of wings, thighs, legs and breasts.

 # LAMB

Lamb is one of my favourite meats, and although it can be expensive, it is normally good quality, so you are getting what you pay for. Some of the tougher parts of the lamb are the most delicious when braised or cooked slowly. Choose meat with a bright red colour – it should never be grey – with fat that is creamy white and firm, and skin that is dry. Lamb has always been cooked on special occasions in my house and these particular cuts are really delicious and my absolute favourites:

Lamb neck
This cut comes from the top of the neck and is most commonly used in soups and stews. Like many cuts from the fore end of the animal, this cut requires slow cooking. It is inexpensive and ideal cut into rough chunks for Irish stew.

Lamb shanks
Lamb shanks have come back into fashion in recent years and as a result their price has increased. So while this is possibly not the cheapest cut, it is still one of my favourites; shanks make a comforting dinner when slowly braised in a rich sauce.

Lamb shoulder
This can be cooked on the bone, or boned, stuffed and rolled. It requires low and slow cooking in the oven. Cooking it on the bone gives it a lovely, rich flavour.

Lamb breast
Lamb breast is a cut that requires a little love and care. It is quite fatty, so needs long, slow roasting to make the meat wonderfully tender.

Lamb kidneys
Unlike pork kidneys, lamb kidneys have a milder flavour and don't require as much work. They can be fried for a tasty little dinner.

Lamb liver
Cooking with offal is a good frugal practice and lamb livers are cheap to buy. Use them gently pan-fried or sliced in rich, creamy sauces.

 # FISHMONGER

The skills offered by fishmongers are invaluable to the home cook; unless you have been trained in filleting fish, doing it yourself at home can be daunting. Your fishmonger will happily gut whole fish and remove any skin or bones if you ask.

Buying the whole fish can often be more economical than just buying fillets. Different varieties of fish are in season at different times and quite often the fish you were planning to buy may not be available, in which case tell your fishmonger which dish you wanted to cook and he may be able to suggest an alternative. Fish is incredibly versatile and can often be swapped for other species. Choose the right fish for your dish, though: oily species can take stronger flavours like garlic and chilli and are suited to barbecuing or grilling, while white fish is more suited to lighter, simpler flavours. In most cases, fish is often best cooked very simply and seasoned with nothing more than sea salt, ground black pepper and a squeeze of lemon juice.

When selecting fish, look for bright, shiny eyes, red gills, firm flesh and, most of all, a fresh sea smell. If you do buy fillets, make sure to choose ones with no signs

of discoloration on the flesh. Fish is always best enjoyed fresh, and unless you are going to freeze it, which can be done quite successfully (see page 19), you should always aim to cook fish on the day you buy it. However, it can keep in the fridge for up to 2 days.

In recent years, the sustainability of fish has become an incredibly important issue, and with world fish stocks depleting, it's imperative to know which species are sustainable and to try to eat more of them and less of the endangered ones. The good news is that many of the sustainable species are actually some of the most inexpensive ones.

GREENGROCER

While it is fantastic that we're able to buy all sorts of different ingredients from around the world, it has become necessary to re-emphasise seasonality. Learning to buy fruit and vegetables that are in season is not only an economical practice but an environmental one, too. In a society where supermarkets have the same produce in stock all year round, it's important to bear in mind what is actually growing at any particular time. Use the seasonality chart overleaf to choose ingredients at their very best.

GROWING YOUR OWN

I've been growing my own vegetables for the past few years and at last feel confident enough to write a little advice for those considering embarking on the process. You don't need much room or equipment to grow your own: just some space and a few bags of soil, but this small investment will save you buying expensive bags of salads and pots of herbs in the supermarket. Since I started, I've moved my veggie patch from a small apartment balcony to a temporary plot in my aunt's back garden, and finally to a back garden of my own.

Even though I have a bit more space these days, if I had known back then what I do now, I could have grown enough on my balcony over the summer to have saved a packet on buying salad leaves and other quick-cropping vegetables. One of the biggest lessons I've learnt is to only plant things you definitely plan to eat and don't go crazy (one year I had 25 cabbages: we ate a lot of coleslaw...!). If, like me, you have no patience, you will also want to choose vegetables that grow quickly. This will keep you interested and you can continue sowing throughout the summer to ensure you have plenty to eat. Although I love the idea that you can be completely self-sufficient, I do have a realistic take on this and my aim is just to grow things that will complement the type of cooking and eating I do in my kitchen. I always try to grow a few new veggies each year but the big winners, in terms of reliability and everyday usage in my kitchen, are those I've listed overleaf...

Salad leaves

If you choose to grow nothing else, it must be salad leaves. They grow in just a few weeks and if you plant enough you won't be able to keep up with them throughout the summer. Rocket and spinach are ideal as you can cut as many leaves as you need and they will continue to grow back until you want them again. Bigger heads of lettuce can take a little longer to grow (and always get obliterated by slugs in my garden!), so rocket and spinach are the safest bet for the first-time grower.

Peas

Garden peas are possibly the most rewarding thing you can grow in the garden; they grow quickly and the taste of peas sampled fresh from the pod is one of the greatest benefits of growing your own. Sow a few peas directly in the ground each week, from late spring and early summer onwards, and you will have a great supply throughout the season – just make sure you give them something to grow up. You can also use the baby shoots as an elegant garnish for salads and other dishes.

Herbs

Herbs were the first things that I started growing and are most definitely the easiest. A must for any home cook, they take very little work and save you buying those supermarket pots or, even worse, those pre-packed bags of soggy herbs. Some of the more hardy herbs are completely failsafe, such as rosemary, thyme, parsley, sage, bay and mint, which can all be popped outside to grow throughout the summer. After dying down in the winter, these herbs will come back with a vengeance in the spring. More delicate herbs, such as basil, coriander and flat-leaf parsley, need a little more love and care, and in my experience grow quite happily on an indoor windowsill. You can buy packets of seeds for herbs or buy established plants from good garden centres.

Cabbages

I love this bulky vegetable and it is one of the few garden monsters that I grow. It does need a little more space and you have to keep an eye on demon slugs, who like to hide amongst the leaves, munching away. There are lots of different varieties, and most are quite reliable to grow. I've had great success with red cabbage, Dutch cabbage and Chinese cabbage. They are great finely sliced in salads, steamed as a side dish for meat or tossed through a stir-fry for a nice bite.

Potatoes

Where would we be without the potato? In recent years, we Irish have been eating less and less of the vegetable that is long ingrained in our history, probably because of its association with rich comfort food. But I see nothing wrong with that, so potatoes are one of my favourite things to grow and incredibly satisfying to dig up.

Edible flowers

I think sometimes there is too much fuss when it comes to food presentation, and so for years I turned my nose up at the idea of edible flowers. However, I finally gave in and grew some in my garden last year; not only did they completely take over the plot, but they also made a really nice addition to summer salads with their great peppery taste. My favourites are nasturtiums.

Asian greens

My best discovery while growing my own has been Asian greens, which grow quite quickly and very easily. They don't need too much care and make wonderful additions to salads and stir-fries. Try sowing pak choi and Chinese cabbage.

Strawberries

A total summer treat, strawberries are easy to grow, and if you plant enough you should get a nice crop of berries in June. The only thing to worry about is birds getting to those berries before you do!

SEASONAL PRODUCE

Spring

Asparagus/ Beetroot/ Broccoli/ Cabbage/ Carrots/ Cauliflower/ Celeriac/ Lettuce/ Spinach

Summer

Beetroot/ Blueberries/ Broad beans/ Carrots/ Cauliflower/ Celery/ Courgettes/ French beans/ Gooseberries/ Mangetout/ Pak choi/ Peas/ Peppers/ Potatoes/ Raspberries/ Rhubarb/ Shallots/ Spinach/ Strawberries/ Swede/ Tomatoes/ Turnips

Autumn

Apples/ Beetroot/ Blackberries/ Carrots/ Cauliflower/ Celeriac/ Celery/ Courgettes/ Leeks/ Onions/ Pak choi/ Parsnips/ Peppers/ Potatoes/ Pumpkin/ Spinach/ Squash/ Swede/ Sweetcorn/ Tomatoes/ Turnips

Winter

Beetroot/ Brussels sprouts/ Carrots/ Cauliflower/ Celeriac/ Jerusalem artichokes/ Kale/ Leeks/ Parsnips

frugal COOKING PRACTICES

Your daily bread

One of the most satisfying kitchen practices is making bread – although shop-bought bread can be a cheap ingredient, making it yourself is delicious, easy and extremely inexpensive. The quick soda bread recipe I've included in the baking chapter (see page 192) doesn't need to rise and is a wonderful alternative to a commercial sliced loaf.

Freezing

The freezer can save you time and money and gives you a ready supply of ingredients to hand. Many foods take well to being frozen and you can also freeze whole dishes, ready to defrost and reheat on demand. If you use your freezer regularly, get a permanent marker so that you can label containers with the date of freezing. Do a clearout every 6 months and use up anything that has been sitting there too long. The best way to defrost food is to put it on a plate in the fridge overnight, but if you are using it straight away once defrosted, simply take it out of the freezer and leave it at room temperature. Foods that don't freeze well are vegetables with a high water content, like lettuce and cabbage, or foods with a creamy base, which can split as they defrost.

> Fruit

Lots of fruit can be frozen: berries in particular freeze well and I keep a steady supply for desserts, baking and smoothies. Some of the best free fruit can be picked from hedgerows, such as blackberries – brush away bugs or dirt or give them a quick rinse before drying them and packing into resealable bags. To keep their shape, freeze berries on trays, cover with cling film and bag them up when frozen. If I find myself with a glut of lemons or oranges I zest them and pop it into bags. Grated zest is excellent in baking recipes, such as muffins and cakes, as well as savoury dishes.

> Vegetables

Not all vegetables freeze well, but some do. Frozen peas are the ultimate freezer standby because, unless you grow them yourself, the process commercial peas go through once picked actually keeps them fresher than the fresh peas you can buy. Frozen spinach is another handy one; it's inexpensive and can be added to recipes, or served as a quick side dish. Mashed potatoes freeze well in bags – just don't add cream to them. I also freeze soft herbs like basil, finely chopped, mixed with a little oil and placed in ice-cube trays. These are great for drizzling over bread dough, or added to soups and sauces for a special hit of flavour.

> Meat

One of the biggest time-savers in my freezer is marinated meat, which happily sits until you are ready to use it. Freezing meat in a marinade can actually heighten the flavours. Another great economical tip is that if you find a good price on a certain cut, make sure to buy extra, which can be frozen. Cooked meat also freezes well; chicken and ham can be chopped up and frozen, then defrosted when needed and mixed through pasta, risotto, or even used in pies and curries.

> Eggs

Recipes often call for egg yolks only. Don't throw out those egg whites: they freeze perfectly and can be stockpiled in resealable freezer bags until you have enough to make meringues! Make sure to keep a note of how many egg whites you have frozen so that you can easily pull out the amount you need. If you do have leftover yolks, these are better suited to storing in the fridge for up to 4 days in a resealable container.

> Fish

Fish freezes well, but bear in mind that oily fish such as mackerel will keep for less time (about 3 months) in the freezer than white fish fillets.

> Wine

Both white and red wine can be frozen, so rather than throwing dregs of bottles down the drain, pour into freezer bags or ice-cube trays. The cubes can then be added to sauces to give a rich flavour.

> Butter wrappers

Call me crazy, but I save these in the freezer, then take them out and warm them between my hands to use for greasing baking tins. Genius or OCD, you decide!

> Soups

Soups freeze extremely well. Make sure your soup is chilled before you place it in the freezer, though, as this will help preserve the texture and flavour. Soups that have been blitzed smooth may split after being defrosted. Don't panic; just mix them back together using a whisk.

> Parmesan rinds

Leftover Parmesan rinds can be saved in the freezer to be added to soups, stews and sauces for an extra-rich taste.

WASTE NOT, WANT NOT:
SAVING LEFTOVERS

Leftovers are an essential ingredient in the armoury of any good home cook.
Knowing how to use them will not only save you money but it also means less waste.
If you cook on a daily basis, leftover food is an inevitability. From time to time, you
may also find yourself left with a bulk amount of one particular ingredient. Knowing
what to do with it is important. Here are some of my best tips for using up leftover
food and ingredients.

Bread

We've all seen what happens to a piece of bread after a week. When I was in school,
I had a science project all about mouldy sandwiches; needless to say I didn't sample
the results! However, that mould can be avoided, as bread freezes extremely well,
so if you have a loaf that you know you won't get through, cut it into slices, wrap
them in cling film and foil and pop in the freezer. You can then pull out slices and
put them straight in the toaster. Bread dough also freezes well – simply follow all the
usual stages and after punching down the dough once it's risen, you can put it in a

resealable bag and place in the freezer. To use, simply allow to defrost, then shape the dough and bake in a hot oven. Many recipes call for breadcrumbs and it seems crazy to go out and buy them when you can simply whizz up stale bread in a food processor (or if it's hard enough you can grate it – a tip from my granny!), pop in a resealable bag and into the freezer for when you need breadcrumbs. Dry bread can also be used for desserts and my mom's Bread and Butter Orchard Pud (see page 175) is an ideal use for it.

Fruit

Leftover fruit can be used for a variety of dishes. Blackening bananas are ideal for baking; bumped and bruised apples and pears make wonderful pies and tarts; and even the most sorry-looking fruits can be whizzed into healthy juices. Fruit is best used in season and I often find myself with a glut of fruits like strawberries from the garden or blackberries from the hedgerows close to my house. They make great additions to seasonal desserts and are fantastic in jams. I also freeze them for smoothies: brush off any dirt or give them a quick rinse and let them dry before storing in resealable freezer bags. There's no better kick-start to the day than a handful of frozen berries blitzed with a banana and apple juice in a refreshing smoothie.

Vegetables

Don't disregard those seemingly lifeless vegetables at the bottom of the fridge: they can be transformed into something beautiful and my first instinct is always to make soup. With a good base of onions and a couple of carrots, you have the beginnings of a warming and worthwhile soup.

The more you cook on a regular basis, the less you need to follow recipes as strictly as before. At this point, you can start putting that kitchen intuition to work and realise that if you are making a bolognaise sauce, for example, you could of course add in a finely chopped carrot, to make use of it. Or use a shallot instead of an onion, or vice versa. The point is to not let those veggies go to waste, thereby saving yourself money.

Meat

Leftover meat can be used in so many different dishes and really is one of the most versatile and handy ingredients. Leftover chicken, beef, lamb and more can help make a meal out of a frittata, salad, pie or stir-fry.

EVERYDAY EASY BAKING

SUPPERS PASTA

SIMPLE SIDES CHEAP &

HEALTHY

☞ SLOW-COOKED MEALS

SOUPS & STEWS DESSERTS

№1

While I love the simplicity of a super-quick pasta dish or an easy Asian stir-fry, my favourite type of cooking takes place on the weekends when I have time to spare. It usually comes in the form of a big, hefty pot, blipping away on the hob or slowly baking in the oven. The result is tender meat in a rich, dark sauce that has benefited from the love and care you put in at the start and its long, slow cooking time.

Soups and stews will always be what I turn to when in search of comfort. It all started when I was very young and first tried Irish stew on a cold and cosy winter's day, when the heat from the kitchen had made all the windows fog up. Many of the soups in this chapter have a bit of substance to them, using grains and pulses to bulk them out, so as my granddad would say, 'there's a bit of eatin' and drinkin' in them'!

The true beauty and cleverness of this particular type of cooking, as any good cook will know, is that you can transform the most inexpensive cuts of meat or unassuming ingredients into something fairly spectacular with very little work. Growing up, I was always amazed at my mom's ability to feed a crowd with ease. Little did I know back then that the real secret to it was the preparation she'd done in advance, which made things run so smoothly. The star of most of her meals was in the oven well before dinner time, slowly cooking away, leaving only side dishes to worry about before guests arrived. I was always drafted in to serve up, but I didn't mind – I was happy to enter into a bit of child labour in exchange for some trade secrets.

Most of the cuts of meat I have included in this chapter should only be cooked slowly and gently until they are tender and moist. If you aren't familiar with cuts like shoulder of pork, ham hock, pork belly, beef skirt or chuck steak, don't be put off: these recipes make them really worth trying and will result in truly delicious dinners. Some of these cuts of meat are pricier than others, but all are good value and will feed a large number of people. The dishes are satisfying and filling, so a little goes a long way.

VIETNAMESE POACHED CHICKEN
NOODLE SOUP

The key to any chicken soup is the broth, and this Vietnamese-inspired Pho Ga chicken noodle soup is no different. Charring the ginger and onion does sound rather an unnecessary undertaking, but it's this step, along with the addition of toasted spices, that makes it a beautifully rich and aromatic broth. Before you place the chicken in the pot to boil, make sure to expose some of the bones by partially cutting the wings with sharp scissors; this makes for an excellent flavour. Slurping is a completely necessary part of devouring this soup!

 **SERVES 6–8**

1 large onion, peeled and sliced in half

2 large, thumb-sized pieces of fresh ginger, peeled and sliced in half

4 cloves

2 star anise

3 tbsp coriander seeds

1 free-range organic chicken (about 1.2kg/2½lb), wing bones exposed

3 tbsp Thai fish sauce (Nam Pla)

300g (11oz) rice noodles

Small handful each of fresh mint, basil and coriander

½ red onion, peeled and finely sliced wafer-thin

Bunch of spring onions, finely sliced

1 red chilli, deseeded and finely sliced

2 limes, cut into quarters

Sea salt

Place the onion halves and ginger pieces on a grill tray and place under a hot grill to char on all sides. The onion should become slightly soft and caramelised.

Meanwhile, toast the cloves, star anise and coriander seeds in a dry frying pan until they become fragrant and aromatic.

Remove the onions and ginger from the grill and add to a large, 9 litre (16 pint) cooking pot, along with the chicken and toasted cloves, star anise and coriander seeds. Cover with cold water and bring to the boil. Simmer for 50 minutes or until the chicken is cooked all the way through. Turn off the heat and leave the chicken to cool in the liquid.

Lift out the chicken from the liquid, remove its skin and shred the meat. Bring the liquid in the pot back to the boil and then lower the heat, add the fish sauce and simmer for a further 40 minutes until the flavour has intensified. Season with sea salt to taste.

Strain the broth through a fine sieve and skim any fat from the top once it has settled. Place the broth back in the pot and bring to the boil. Add the rice noodles and cook until soft.

Serve the noodles and broth in deep bowls, topped with the shredded chicken, the mint, basil and coriander leaves, slices of red onion and spring onion, red chilli and a wedge of lime.

ANGIE'S SKEHAN FAMILY
IRISH STEW

Angie looked after my dad when he was growing up, and when I first started going to school she used to walk me home and give me lunch, which was regularly Irish stew. Her Irish stew is legendary in the Skehan family, with my dad's five siblings and my eleven cousins all having been brought up on it. Angie always knew how to feed an army of hungry mouths, so I hope this version of the recipe does hers justice!

 SERVES 6

2 tbsp rapeseed oil

1kg (2lb 3oz) lamb shoulder, trimmed and cut into 2.5cm (1in) chunks

2 onions, peeled and roughly chopped

3 celery stalks, trimmed and roughly chopped

4 large carrots, peeled and roughly chopped

1 bay leaf

1 litre (1¼ pints) beef or lamb stock

900g (2lb) potatoes, peeled and cut into 1cm (½in) slices

Good knob of butter

Sea salt and ground black pepper

Slices of white bread, to serve

Place a large, flameproof casserole pot over a high heat, add 1 tablespoon of the oil and brown the lamb pieces in two batches. Remove and set aside on a plate.

Reduce the heat to medium–high, add another tablespoon of oil and fry the onions, celery and carrots for 4–6 minutes or until the onions have softened.

Preheat the oven to 160°C (325°F), Gas Mark 3. Return the meat to the pot, along with the bay leaf and stock, season with sea salt and ground black pepper and bring to the boil.

Remove from the heat and push the slices of potato down into and across the top of the stew, dot with a little butter and give a final seasoning of sea salt and ground black pepper. Cover and place in the oven to cook for about 1½ hours or until the meat is tender, then remove the lid and cook for a further 10 minutes until the potatoes have coloured.

You can serve the stew straight away or leave it covered overnight in the fridge for the flavours to develop. Serve in deep bowls with slices of white bread to soak up the liquid.

CHINESE FIVE-SPICE
PORK BELLY

Crispy crackling and tender pork belly meat paired with Chinese five-spice powder – a match made in heaven. For just the tiniest amount of work in the kitchen, using an inexpensive piece of meat, you get the most amazing results, which will feed a crowd. There are many different things you can do with pork belly as it's quite versatile, but I like the simplicity of this method; it's a nod to Asia, where this is an incredibly popular cut of meat.

🐖 SERVES 6

2kg (4½lb) pork belly, fat scored horizontally

3 tbsp rapeseed oil

1–2 tsp Chinese five-spice powder

2 garlic bulbs, peeled and sliced in half horizontally

1 large onion, peeled and cut into thick slices horizontally

Sea salt

Asian Greens (see page 134) and sugar snap peas, to serve

Preheat the oven to 160°C (325°F), Gas Mark 3. Rub the pork belly all over with oil, dust with the Chinese five-spice powder and sprinkle with sea salt.

Place the garlic bulb halves and onion slices in the base of a large roasting tin and place the pork belly on top, flesh-side down. Pour in a few tablespoons of water. Cover with tinfoil and put the roasting tin in the oven and cook for 2½–3 hours.

Turn up the oven to 220°C (425°F), Gas Mark 7, remove the tinfoil and cook the pork for a further 15–20 minutes until the skin is crispy. Carve into thick slices and serve with wilted Asian greens and sugar snap peas.

MUM'S COQ AU VIN BLANC

Coq au vin blanc was a regular winter dish in my house when we were growing up. I have memories of it steaming up the kitchen windows while we did our homework on the kitchen table. It's a wonderfully warming meal, perfect for cold evenings. Chicken joints such as thighs and legs are often far cheaper to buy than chicken breasts, and meat cooked on the bone always has more flavour.

SERVES 4

1 tbsp olive oil

4 chicken legs

15g (½oz) butter

150g (5oz) bacon or pancetta pieces

2 garlic cloves, peeled and finely chopped

1 large onion, peeled and finely chopped

200g (7oz) mushrooms (about 10-15 mushrooms), sliced into quarters

2 fresh thyme sprigs

450ml (16fl oz) white wine (about 2 glasses)

250ml (9fl oz) single cream

Good handful of freshly chopped flat-leaf parsley

Sea salt and ground black pepper

Place a large cooking pot over a high heat and add the olive oil. Put the chicken legs in the pot and brown on all sides until they are a golden colour. Remove and set aside on a plate.

Reduce the heat slightly and add the butter. When it begins to foam, add the bacon and fry until just crisp. Add the garlic and onion and fry for 3-4 minutes. Add the mushrooms and cook for a further 3 minutes.

Return the chicken to the pot along with the thyme and pour in the white wine. Bring to the boil and simmer over a low heat for 45-50 minutes or until the chicken is cooked all the way through. Turn the legs halfway through the cooking time and remove any fat or scum that rises to the top.

When the chicken is cooked, remove from the pot and set aside. Stir the cream into the juices, add a good pinch of sea salt and black pepper and simmer for a further 10 minutes or until the sauce has become a little thicker.

Place the chicken back in the pot to allow it to warm through and stir through the chopped parsley. Make sure the food is hot when you serve it at the table.

ROASTED TOMATO & GARLIC SOUP

A good tomato soup is a fantastic recipe to have in your repertoire. By roasting the tomatoes for this soup you end up with really intense flavours, and even if you can't get your hands on the best tomatoes, roasting really transforms them into something special.

 SERVES 4 (V)

900g (2lb) tomatoes, sliced in half

2 garlic bulbs, tops sliced off

1 tbsp balsamic vinegar

2 tbsp olive oil

4 large thyme sprigs, leaves picked off

1 large onion, peeled and finely sliced

2 celery stalks, trimmed and finely chopped

1 carrot, peeled and finely chopped

2 tbsp tomato purée

1 litre (1¾ pints) vegetable stock

Sea salt and ground black pepper

Crusty bread and extra-virgin olive oil, to serve

Preheat the oven to 200°C (400°F), Gas Mark 6. Lay the tomatoes cut-side up in a large roasting tin and nuzzle the garlic bulbs in with them. (Make sure to use a big-enough roasting tin to allow the tomatoes to roast rather than stew – if it's too small they won't caramelise on the outsides. If required, use two roasting tins and swap shelves in the oven halfway through the cooking time.) Drizzle with the balsamic vinegar and 1 tablespoon of olive oil. Sprinkle with the thyme leaves, sea salt and ground black pepper.

Place in the oven and roast for 45 minutes or until the tomatoes have shrunk and are slightly caramelised on the outside and the garlic is soft and mushy. Remove from the oven and set aside while you prepare the base of the soup.

Place a large cooking pot over a high heat and add the remaining 1 tablespoon of olive oil. Add the onion, celery and carrot and fry for 1 minute, stirring every now and then. Reduce the heat to medium and cook for 6 minutes until tender. Add the tomato purée and stock and bring to a steady simmer.

Squeeze the cloves from the roasted garlic bulbs and add them to the soup, along with the roasted tomatoes and their juices. Simmer for 25 minutes until the carrot is completely tender. Season to taste with sea salt and ground black pepper. Using a hand blender or in a food processor, blitz the soup until completely smooth.

Serve the soup warm in deep bowls with some crusty bread and drizzle a little extra-virgin olive oil on the top.

MOROCCAN SPICED
LAMB SHOULDER

My first memories of lamb shoulder are of the amazing aroma coming from my granny's oven one Sunday morning when I was young. I was so curious about what could possibly be cooking in the oven to create such a tantalising smell. My granny – always eager to encourage my taste buds – sliced off a chunk, much to my granddad's horror, and sent me home with it. It didn't get that far, because I unwrapped it in the back seat on the car ride home and guzzled the lot! Lamb shoulder really needs to be cooked at a low heat for a long period of time to make the most of it. This spiced version is delicious, but for a more traditional flavour you could simply stud the lamb with garlic and rosemary.

 SERVES 6

2 tbsp olive oil

2 tsp ground ginger

2 tsp ground cumin

2 tsp ground coriander

2 tsp ground turmeric

Grated zest and juice
of 1 lemon

Small bunch of coriander,
leaves picked and stalks
roughly chopped

1.5kg (3lb 5oz) lamb
shoulder

Sea salt and ground
black pepper

Couscous and lemon
wedges, to serve

Preheat the oven to 160°C (325°F), Gas Mark 3.

Place the olive oil, ginger, cumin, ground coriander, turmeric, lemon zest and juice, chopped coriander stalks and a good pinch of salt into a mini blender. Blitz to form a smooth paste, or use a pestle and mortar.

Put the lamb shoulder onto two large pieces of foil and make lots of incisions in the meat with a knife. Rub the paste all over. Add a couple of tablespoons of water, then seal the foil around the lamb, leaving a little pocket of air above it. Place on a baking sheet and cook for 4 hours.

After this time, open the foil and baste the lamb with its juices. Leaving the foil open, cook for a further hour, by which time the lamb should be meltingly tender. Turn off the oven but leave the lamb inside to rest.

Serve in slices with plain couscous (or you can add some chickpeas and possibly feta for extra flavour and texture, see page 153) garnished with coriander leaves, as a tasty spring/summer Sunday dinner, with a lemon wedge on the side.

CHEESY
POTATO TART

Don't underestimate this little potato tart – it's quite a sophisticated dish. It reminds me of the type of cooking my grandmother and I have long conversations about, using frugal ingredients and basic cooking methods to achieve wonderful results. Any type of cheese works well, such as Brie, Gruyère, Cheddar or blue.

☛ SERVES 6–8

For the shortcrust pastry

200g (7oz) plain flour, plus extra for dusting

100g (3½oz) butter, very cold and cut into cubes, plus extra for greasing

2 tbsp ice-cold water

For the filling

1 tbsp rapeseed oil

400g (14oz) waxy potatoes, peeled and thinly sliced

1 large onion, peeled and thinly sliced

150g (5oz) cheese, grated or crumbled

½ tsp chopped fresh thyme

200ml (7fl oz) cream

3 large free-range eggs

Pinch of nutmeg

Sea salt and ground black pepper

Put the flour and butter into a mixing bowl and, using your fingertips, lightly rub them together until the mixture looks like breadcrumbs. Stir in the cold water a little at a time and incorporate with a spoon. When the dough comes together, turn out onto a clean work surface and knead lightly just until it forms a ball. Press into a flat circle, wrap in cling film and allow to rest in the fridge for 30 minutes.

Grease a 23cm (8in) pie dish, 4cm (1½ in) in depth (capacity 1.2 litres /2 pints), and dust with flour. Roll out the dough into a circle on a clean, floured work surface, to about 5mm (¼in) thick.

Transfer the rolled-out pastry to the tin and gently press it into all the sides. Roughly trim off most of the excess but leave some all round the edge of the tin to allow for shrinking. Don't panic if the pastry breaks at all, just press it together with your fingers and repair any cracks with a little of the trimmed pastry. Chill in the fridge for 10–15 minutes.

Preheat the oven to 180°C (350°F), Gas Mark 4. Prick the pastry base with a fork, line with some scrunched-up greaseproof paper and pour in baking beans or dried pulses. Place in the oven for 15 minutes, then remove the greaseproof paper and beans and cook for a further 5 minutes until lightly golden. Remove from the oven, trim off the remaining excess pastry and set aside on a wire cooling rack.

Meanwhile, place a large frying pan over a high heat, add the oil and fry the potatoes and onion for 20–25 minutes until tender, stirring regularly to ensure they don't stick. Mix through the cheese and thyme and arrange on the base of the pastry case.

Whisk together the cream and eggs, season with nutmeg, sea salt and ground black pepper. Pour this over the potatoes, making sure it gets into all the nooks and crannies. Place the tart in the oven to cook for about 20 minutes, until golden on top and set.

BAKED SMOKED
HADDOCK & POTATOES

This all-in-one potato and fish dish makes a filling supper for friends. Serve it straight away with a big bowl of dressed salad leaves for some inexpensive entertaining.

 SERVES 6

50g (2oz) butter, plus extra for greasing

700g (1½lb) waxy potatoes, peeled and sliced wafer-thin

500g (1lb 2oz) smoked haddock fillets, skinned and boned, cut into 2.5cm (1in) chunks

180g (6½oz) frozen peas

2 garlic cloves, peeled and finely chopped

Good handful of dill, freshly chopped

200ml (7fl oz) cream

Ground black pepper

Preheat the oven to 180°C (350°F), Gas Mark 4 and grease a roasting tin with butter.

In a large mixing bowl, gently toss together the potatoes, fish, peas, garlic and dill.

Arrange the contents of the bowl in the roasting tin and pour over the cream. Press everything down with your hands so that the cream soaks through.

Dot the top with little knobs of the butter and give it a good grinding of black pepper.

Roast in the oven for 45 minutes until the top is golden and the potatoes are tender when pierced with a fork.

SLOW-COOKED
MEATY CHILLI

Hearty food like this meaty chilli makes me very happy inside; it's full of great spices and filling ingredients, and best of all it feeds a crowd. Using finely chopped meat here rather than mince gives a really interesting texture to the chilli.

☞ SERVES 4–6

2 tbsp rapeseed oil

1 large onion, peeled and finely chopped

3 garlic cloves, peeled and finely chopped

3 small carrots, peeled and finely chopped

2 celery stalks, trimmed and finely chopped

2 red peppers, deseeded and finely chopped

2 tsp chilli powder

1 tsp smoked paprika

2 tsp ground cumin

500g (1lb 2oz) rib steak, finely chopped

2 x 400g (14oz) tins of chopped tomatoes

1 tbsp Worcestershire sauce

1 tbsp treacle

1 x 400g (14oz) tin each of kidney beans and chickpeas, drained and rinsed

Sea salt and ground black pepper

Crusty bread or tortilla chips, crème fraîche and/or coriander leaves, to serve

Place a large cooking pot or flameproof casserole pan over a medium-high heat and add the oil. Add the onion, garlic, carrots, celery and peppers. Then stir through the spices – the chilli powder, smoked paprika and cumin. Fry the mixture for 7–8 minutes until the vegetables are tender.

Add the meat to the pan and fry gently until lightly browned, stirring regularly. Pour in the chopped tomatoes and then fill both the tins with hot water and pour this in also. Add the Worcestershire sauce and treacle.

Pour in the kidney beans and chickpeas, bring the mixture to the boil, then reduce the heat and simmer for about 30 minutes, stirring every now and then.

When the chilli has reduced, season with sea salt and ground black pepper. Serve in deep bowls with crusty bread or tortilla chips, a dollop of crème fraîche and coriander leaves, if you wish.

RIBOLLITA

Ribollita is a traditional Italian peasant soup that makes an ideal base for ingredients that you want to use up. Think of it as an opportunity to give a last moment of glory to any miserable veggies left at the bottom of your fridge! I keep leftover Parmesan rinds in my freezer, which I add to sauces and soups to give a unique, rich flavour. Add a couple while the soup is simmering then fish them out before serving.

☞ SERVES 6–8

1 tbsp rapeseed oil

150g (5oz) smoked streaky bacon, finely chopped

2 red onions, peeled and finely chopped

4 carrots, peeled and finely chopped

4 celery stalks, trimmed and finely chopped

4 garlic cloves, peeled and finely chopped

1 tsp red chilli flakes

2 x 400g (14oz) tins of whole plum tomatoes

½ head of Savoy cabbage, shredded

1.5 litres (2½ pints) chicken or vegetable stock

1 bay leaf

1–2 leftover Parmesan rinds (optional)

3 large handfuls of sourdough bread, cut into cubes

1 x 400g (14oz) tin of cannellini beans, drained and rinsed

50g (2oz) Parmesan cheese, finely grated

Sea salt and ground black pepper

Good-quality extra-virgin olive oil, to serve

Heat the oil in a large cooking pot over a medium heat, add the bacon and onions and fry until the onions are tender. Add the carrots, celery, garlic and chilli flakes and stir through, cooking for a further 5–6 minutes or until the carrots are tender.

Pour in the plum tomatoes and use a potato masher to quickly break them up, then add the shredded cabbage and cook for a further 5 minutes.

Pour in the stock, add the bay leaf and any leftover Parmesan rinds you might have, then bring to the boil. Reduce the heat and simmer for 15 minutes. Season with sea salt and ground black pepper.

Add the cubes of bread and cannellini beans and cook for a further 6–8 minutes until the bread has softened and thickened the soup. Serve in deep bowls, sprinkled with grated Parmesan and drizzled with extra-virgin olive oil.

SIMPLE BOILED
HAM HOCK

I think it's the cheapskate in me that gets so much satisfaction from the amount of meat you get from a ham hock for such a small price. Sure, there's a little bit of work involved in boiling and shredding the meat, but it results in a really versatile ingredient that can be added to lots of dishes. It is worth boiling more than one hock at a time – any meat you don't use right away freezes well and is easy to defrost when you want it. I love adding the shredded meat to salads, crêpes, fried rice, frittatas, stir-fries and much more. It can also be made into an elegant terrine and served as a sophisticated starter. If you're planning to put the meat into a soup, save some of the liquid the ham hocks were boiled in, to use in place of stock.

 **PRODUCES ABOUT**
500G/1LB 2OZ
COOKED MEAT

2 ham hocks
(each about 900g/2lb)

Place the ham hocks in a large, heavy-based pan, cover with cold water and bring to the boil, skimming off any foam that rises to the surface.

Reduce the heat and simmer for about 45 minutes or until the meat pulls away from the bone. The cooking time will depend on the piece of meat, so check it with a fork; the meat is cooked when it is tender and easy to loosen from the bone.

Remove the pan from the heat and allow the ham to cool in the water. When the meat is cool, remove from the pan and remove the outer skin, then use a fork to shred the meat from the bone.

You can use the cooked meat immediately or freeze it in resealable bags for up to 6 months.

SLOW-COOKED STEAK &
GUINNESS PIE

If you want, you can serve this as a stew and skip the step of adding the pastry, but I love the look of this pie when it comes out of the oven. Crispy, flaky pastry with meaty juices bubbling up the sides … delicious! If after simmering the sauce isn't thick enough for your liking, combine equal small amounts of flour and melted butter and whisk into the sauce to thicken.

SERVES 6

1–2 tbsp rapeseed oil

1kg (2lb 3oz) beef shoulder, cut into 2.5cm (1in) chunks

1 onion, peeled and roughly chopped

2 carrots, peeled and roughly chopped

2 celery stalks, trimmed and roughly chopped

2 garlic cloves, peeled and finely sliced

150ml (5fl oz) beef stock

500ml (18fl oz) Guinness

1 bay leaf

1 egg, beaten

1 ready-rolled sheet of puff pastry

Sea salt and ground black pepper

Heat 1 tablespoon of the oil in a large cooking pot and brown the meat in two batches, being careful not to overcrowd the pan. Remove and set aside on a plate.

Add another tablespoon of oil if you need it and fry the onion, carrots and celery for 6 minutes, until the onion is soft. Return the meat to the pot, along with the garlic. Pour in the stock and Guinness, add the bay leaf and season with sea salt and black pepper to taste. Simmer gently for about 1½ hours until the liquid has reduced and the meat is tender, stirring occasionally to make sure that it doesn't stick.

Preheat the oven to 200°C (400°F), Gas Mark 6. Brush the edges of a 1.2 litre (2 pint) oval baking dish with a little beaten egg, then fill with the beef and Guinness mixture. Top with the sheet of puff pastry, pressing to seal the edges.

Cut one or two holes in the pastry lid to allow steam to escape, then brush all over with beaten egg. Place the pie in the oven to bake for 25–30 minutes, until the pastry has risen and has turned a crisp, golden colour.

CHUCK STEAK
STROGANOFF

Stroganoff is traditionally a Russian dish but because of its popularity across the world it appears in many different incarnations. My version uses chuck steak, which can be tough if cooked too quickly; it benefits from a low and slow cooking until it's nice and tender.

☞ SERVES 6

2 tbsp rapeseed oil

700g (1½lb) lean chuck steak, sliced thinly

30g (1oz) butter

1 large onion, peeled and finely sliced

1 tsp smoked paprika

1 tbsp wholegrain mustard

300ml (10½fl oz) white wine

250g (9oz) small mushrooms, sliced in half

200ml (7fl oz) crème fraîche or soured cream

Sea salt and ground black pepper

Mashed potatoes or rice, to serve

Place a large, high-sided frying pan over a medium–high heat and add 1 tablespoon of the oil. Brown the meat in batches until it has a good colour on all sides, making sure not to overcrowd the pan. After you've browned each batch, transfer to a plate.

Add the butter and another tablespoon of oil to the pan and, when the butter has melted and begun to foam, add the onion and fry for 6–8 minutes until softened and golden. Mix the meat back into the pan, along with the paprika and mustard, then pour in the wine and bring to the boil.

Season with sea salt and ground black pepper, then reduce the heat right down, cover with a lid and cook very gently for 1 hour 15 minutes or until the meat is tender. Every now and then, remove the lid and give the mixture a quick stir to make sure it doesn't stick to the bottom.

After this time, add the mushrooms and crème fraîche and simmer gently for about 10 minutes until the mushrooms are tender. Check the seasoning and add a little extra salt and pepper if necessary. Serve with mashed potatoes or rice.

PORCHETTA

This is definitely one of my favourite recipes. It's made using pork shoulder, an inexpensive cut that, when cooked in this manner, results in wonderfully tender meat and crispy crackling. If the idea of rolling and stringing up the shoulder around the stuffing is too much, take the stuffing with you to the butcher when you buy the meat and ask for it to be stuffed and rolled for you. Then it's simply a case of roasting it.

☞ **SERVES 6–8**

2.75kg (6lb) boneless shoulder of pork, with skin, at room temperature

Small handful of sage leaves

2 rosemary sprigs

4 thyme sprigs

50g (2oz) Parmesan cheese, finely grated

Grated zest of 1 lemon

4 garlic cloves, peeled and finely chopped

1 small onion, peeled and finely chopped

Sea salt and ground black pepper

Root veg mash (see page 136) and spinach, to serve

Preheat the oven to 190°C (375°F), Gas Mark 5. If the shoulder of pork has been tied, cut the strings and open out the meat onto a clean work surface, then season generously with sea salt and ground black pepper.

Remove and discard the stems from the sage leaves, and strip the leaves off the rosemary and thyme sprigs. Finely chop all the leaves, then toss in a bowl with the Parmesan cheese, lemon zest, garlic and onion.

Sprinkle the stuffing mixture over the laid-out pork and then, starting with one side, tightly roll the pork back up to enclose the filling completely. Tie with string at 2cm (¾in) intervals to keep the meat in shape. If the skin is not already scored, use a small, sharp knife to score the skin between the strings. Pat the skin dry with kitchen paper and sprinkle with sea salt.

Place in a roasting tin and roast for 2 hours 20 minutes until cooked through and tender. (If the weight of your pork varies from mine, the rule is to allow 20 minutes per 500g/1lb 2oz, plus an additional 20 minutes.) For the final 20 minutes of cooking time, increase the oven temperature to 220°C (425°F), Gas Mark 7, to produce the crispy crackling.

Leave the roasted pork to rest in a warm place for 30 minutes, as it is actually best served warm. Carve into thin slices and arrange on warmed plates with some root veg mash, spinach and roast potatoes if you like. Spoon over the pan juices to serve.

DAD'S BRAISED
OXTAIL

Anytime you ask my dad about food he always brings up oxtail. I'm fairly sure it would be his Desert Island Dish. When he tried out this recipe, he told me it was 'bloody great', so I think it got his seal of approval! If you haven't cooked oxtail before, the aim is to cook them until the meat just falls off the bone. I serve mine sitting proudly on top of some creamy colcannon mash.

SERVES 4–6

2–3 tbsp plain flour

1 tbsp rapeseed oil

1.8kg (4lb) oxtail

4 red onions, peeled and roughly chopped

4 carrots, peeled and roughly diced

2 celery stalks, trimmed and roughly diced

1 tbsp tomato purée

1 tbsp English mustard powder

2 tbsp Worcestershire sauce

500ml (18fl oz) red wine

400ml (14fl oz) beef stock

4 tbsp balsamic vinegar

2 rosemary sprigs

2 thyme sprigs

Sea salt and ground black pepper

Mashed potato, cooked lentils or steamed veg, to serve

In a bowl, mix the flour with a generous grind of black pepper. Place a large, flameproof casserole pot over a high heat and add most of the oil.

Pat the oxtail dry with a little kitchen paper. Roll the pieces in the seasoned flour and add to the pot one by one. Don't overcrowd the pan, or you won't get a good colour on the meat – do it in two batches if necessary. Brown the oxtail on all sides, turning with tongs, until the meat has a nice colour. Remove from the pan and set aside on a plate.

Preheat the oven to 160°C (325°F), Gas Mark 3. Add an extra drop of oil to the pot, reduce the heat and add the onions, carrots and celery. Fry for 4–6 minutes until just tender. Stir through the tomato purée, mustard powder and Worcestershire sauce until evenly combined.

Pour over the red wine, beef stock and balsamic vinegar and pop in the rosemary and thyme sprigs. Season with sea salt. Cover with a lid and place in the oven to cook slowly for 3½ hours until the meat is just about falling away from the bone.

Serve the braised oxtail and its sauce over mash or lentils, or with some steamed veggies.

ROOT VEG &
BARLEY SOUP

Pearl barley is a totally underrated grain and one that we should all be using more of. It's highly nutritious, costs very little and is extremely versatile. I love adding it to soups like this one or using it to bulk up salads.

☛ SERVES 4–6 (V)

1 tbsp rapeseed oil

15g (½oz) butter

1 onion, peeled and roughly diced

3 celery stalks, trimmed and roughly diced

2 carrots, peeled and roughly diced

1 parsnip, peeled and roughly diced

1 garlic clove, peeled and crushed

200g (7oz) pearl barley

1 litre (1¾ pints) vegetable stock

Sea salt and ground black pepper

Place a large cooking pot over a medium–high heat and add the oil and butter. When it begins to foam, add the onion and fry for 4 minutes until just tender. Add the celery, carrots, parsnip, garlic and pearl barley and mix through for a further 1 minute.

Pour in the vegetable stock and bring to a steady boil for 30–35 minutes until the veggies are tender and the pearl barley has plumped up and become soft.

Top up with water if you find the soup is too thick, season with sea salt and ground black pepper, and serve. (If you plan to keep any of the soup to reheat at a later date, be aware that the pearl barley will continue to soak up liquid, so you may need to add some extra water to compensate.)

BEEF SKIRT GOULASH WITH PAPRIKA SPICED DUMPLINGS

Goulash was one of my mom's regular dinners when I was growing up, and I loved it. The addition of dumplings is my own twist.

 SERVES 4–6

2 tbsp rapeseed oil

675g (1½lb) beef skirt steak pieces

2 large onions, peeled and chopped

1 garlic clove, peeled and chopped

1 heaped tbsp smoked paprika

1 tsp dried oregano

1 heaped tbsp plain flour

2 x 400g (14oz) tins of chopped tomatoes

1 tbsp tomato purée

2 green peppers, deseeded and roughly chopped

3 tbsp soured cream

Sea salt and ground black pepper

Brown rice and steamed veg, to serve

100g (3½oz) very cold butter, in cubes

250g (9oz) self-raising flour

1 tsp smoked paprika

Heat 1 tablespoon of rapeseed oil in a large, flameproof casserole pot and brown the beef on all sides. Make sure not to put too much beef in the pot at once, or it won't brown – it's best to fry it in batches. Transfer the meat to a plate and set aside.

Preheat the oven to 140°C (275°F), Gas Mark 1. Add another tablespoon of oil to the pot if required, then add the onions and garlic and fry until soft and golden, for about 6 minutes.

Return the beef to the pot and stir in the paprika, oregano and flour to coat. Add the tomatoes, tomato purée and a good pinch of sea salt and black pepper, then bring to a steady simmer. Place the lid on the casserole pot and transfer to the oven to cook for about 2 hours.

Thirty minutes before the end of the cooking time, prepare the dumplings by rubbing the butter and flour together in a bowl until the mix resembles fine breadcrumbs. Mix in the paprika and season with sea salt and ground black pepper. Bring the mixture together with a couple of tablespoons of water until you have a dough. Knead slightly, before forming into dumplings each a little smaller than your palm.

Stir the green peppers through the goulash, then arrange the dumplings around the edge of the pot and place back in the oven for 25 minutes until they have turned golden.

Just before serving, stir through a little soured cream to create a wonderful marbled effect. Serve with some freshly cooked brown rice and steamed veggies.

UNCLE FERG'S COWBOY
FRANKS & BEANS

My uncle Fergus is definitely in the 'can't cook, won't cook' category, but his lack of kitchen skills hasn't stopped him from coming up with some great quick fixes. When I stayed over with him once, he made us the only thing he could: some frankfurters chopped up in baked beans then heated up in the microwave! Top-class cooking it was not, but this dish is inspired by him and hopefully it might get people like him into the kitchen. These cowboy franks and beans are true comfort food and full of rich, spicy and sweet flavours. You can also serve them as a beefed-up, beans-on-toast brunch – great with some freshly toasted bread slathered in butter.

SERVES 6

1 tbsp rapeseed oil

3 medium onions, peeled and roughly chopped

3 garlic cloves, peeled and finely chopped

1 tsp smoked paprika

1 tsp cayenne pepper

1-2 rosemary sprigs

3 tbsp treacle

2 x 400g (14oz) tins of chopped tomatoes

250ml (9fl oz) beer (ale) or beef stock

1 tbsp Worcestershire sauce

2 x 400g (14oz) tins of haricot beans, drained and rinsed

8 thick sausages

Sea salt and ground black pepper

Place a medium, flameproof casserole dish over a medium–high heat and add the oil. Fry the onions for 6–8 minutes until they begin to soften and caramelise. Add the garlic, paprika, cayenne, rosemary and treacle and cook for a further 2 minutes.

Pour in the tomatoes, beer and Worcestershire sauce, bring to the boil and season with sea salt and ground black pepper. Reduce the heat and slowly simmer for about 35 minutes until the sauce has reduced. Ten minutes before it has finished cooking, stir through the beans.

While the sauce is cooking, grill or fry the sausages until cooked through with a good colour on all sides. Slice each sausage in three and stir gently into the bean mixture. Check the seasoning and add more salt and pepper if you wish. Serve straight away in deep bowls.

ROASTED SQUASH, COCONUT & CHILLI SOUP

Roasted squash produces wonderful soups with a velvety consistency when blitzed smooth. The addition of coconut milk adds a creamy and exotic flavour, but if you don't want to use it, you could replace it with vegetable stock. This is a warming soup, ideal in autumn and winter.

 **SERVES 4–6 (V)**

1kg (2lb 3oz) butternut squash, peeled and chopped into rough chunks

A few thyme sprigs

2 tbsp rapeseed oil

2 red onions, peeled and roughly chopped

1 tsp red chilli flakes

1 x 400ml (14fl oz) tin of coconut milk

600ml (1 pint) vegetable stock, plus a little extra if required

Sea salt and ground black pepper

Crusty bread, to serve

Preheat the oven to 220°C (425°F), Gas Mark 7. Tumble the squash pieces into a roasting tin with the thyme sprigs and toss them in 1 tablespoon of the oil. Season with sea salt and ground black pepper and pop in the oven to roast for 45 minutes or until the edges are slightly charred and the squash is tender when pierced with a fork.

In a large cooking pot, heat the remaining tablespoon of oil and fry the onions until they are soft. Stir through the chilli flakes and fry for a further minute.

Discard the thyme and add the roasted squash to the pot, along with the coconut milk and vegetable stock. Bring to the boil and simmer for 5 minutes.

Remove the pot from the heat and, using a hand blender, whizz the soup until you have a smooth, velvety consistency. You may need to add more stock or boiling water if it is too thick. Add sea salt and ground black pepper and check the seasoning. Serve the soup in warm bowls with some crusty bread.

RED LENTIL SOUP

This is a wonderfully earthy soup, perfect for cold autumn and winter days, and because of the lentils it's incredibly filling. Play around with the spices here; add them to your liking. It might be nice to add in extras such as smoked streaky bacon, or any leftover ham hock (see page 42).

🖢 SERVES 4–6 (V)

1 tbsp olive oil

1 large onion, peeled and finely chopped

2 celery stalks, trimmed and finely diced

2 carrots, peeled and finely diced

2 garlic cloves, peeled and finely chopped

½ tsp red chilli flakes

1 tsp ground cumin

1 tsp mild curry powder

1 litre (1¾ pints) vegetable stock, plus a little extra if required

200g (7oz) red lentils

Crème fraîche, to serve

Place a large cooking pot over a medium–high heat, add the oil and fry the onion, celery and carrots until tender. Add the garlic, chilli flakes, cumin and curry powder and fry for a further minute.

Pour in the stock, add the lentils and bring to a steady simmer for 25 minutes. By this point, the lentils should have turned to mush. If you like a smoother consistency you can blitz it at this point with a hand blender. If the soup is too thick, add more stock or boiling water until you have the correct consistency.

Season with sea salt and ground black pepper and serve straight away with a dollop of crème fraîche on top.

☞ EVERYDAY EASY SUPPERS

BAKING

PASTA

SIMPLE

SIDES

CHEAP &

HEALTHY

SLOW-COOKED MEALS

SOUPS & STEWS

DESSERTS

Nº2

An important skill in the armoury of any good home cook is the ability to create delicious meals in very little time with just a handful of ingredients. When I first moved out of my parents' house, many of the recipes I had in my repertoire were time-consuming and costly, and certainly not suited to a nine-to-five lifestyle, which required meals that were fast to make and suited a tight budget.

At first it can be difficult to draw quick inspiration from very few ingredients, but when you start what I call 'clever cooking', that can change fairly rapidly. By clever cooking, I mean cooking with leftovers in mind, cooking in the knowledge of what's happening tomorrow or the day after, having a freezer full of little goodies that can easily be defrosted when needed, and of course having a well-stocked storecupboard, filled with simple ingredients that can be the makings of some of the most amazing dishes.

Leftovers were always a sensitive subject when I was growing up, because if you ever mentioned to my mom that you enjoyed a meal, the next time she would make enough to feed an army and you would end up eating it for the entire week! As much as we complained about it while growing up, there was method in her madness. Cooking up a little extra when you are making rice to serve with a curry, or pasta to go with a ragù, will give you the bones of a brand new meal, saving you both time and money.

I do agree that cold rice, or leftovers in general for that matter, can leave you far from inspired in the kitchen, but knowing what to do with them is the first step. The recipes in this chapter capitalise on a well-thought-out kitchen, smart shopping, freezer standbys, leftovers and inexpensive ingredients.

BASIC WHITE WINE & GARLIC
STEAMED MUSSELS

Mussels have a reputation for being difficult to cook, but that's just not true. In reality, the hardest part is washing them. Place in cold water (they should close; if any don't, throw them away). Scrub any dirt off the surface of the mussels and remove the beard with a small knife. If you can get this down, you'll have no further trouble, and they take just minutes to cook, so they're the perfect little starter. I love to serve the cooking pot at the table, clunking large spoonfuls of steaming mussels onto my guests' plates. There are lots of alternatives for this basic recipe: swap out the wine for cider or coconut milk, or replace the pancetta with chorizo.

 SERVES 4

1.5kg (3lb 5oz) mussels, washed and beards removed

100g (7oz) pancetta pieces (or chopped smoked streaky bacon)

Good knob of butter

1 medium onion, peeled and finely chopped

3 garlic cloves, peeled and crushed

½ glass of white wine (about 150ml/5fl oz)

4 tbsp single cream

Good handful of freshly chopped flat-leaf parsley

Sea salt and ground black pepper

Crusty bread, to serve

Immediately discard any mussels that stay open while they are being washed.

Place a large cooking pot over a high heat and brown the pancetta pieces until just golden and sizzling. Add in the knob of butter, allow it to melt, then add the onion and garlic. Cook gently for 3 minutes until the onion is soft.

Pour in the wine and let it bubble away for a few minutes so that all the flavours mingle together. Tumble in the mussels, cover with a lid and allow to steam for about 4 minutes until the mussels open (discard any that remain closed), making sure to give the pot a good shake once or twice during the cooking time.

Remove from the heat, stir in the cream and parsley and season with sea salt and ground black pepper. Serve with some crusty bread to mop up the liquid.

CHILLI JAM
CHICKEN

Chilli jam is an incredibly versatile little condiment and makes a wonderfully sweet and sticky coating for crispy chicken thighs. You can make your own chilli jam very easily – I love to make up big batches of it, transfer it into jars and parcel them up as perfect foodie gifts.

SERVES 4

1 tbsp rapeseed oil

1 tbsp dark soy sauce

1 tbsp rice wine, rice wine vinegar or white wine vinegar

1 large thumb-sized piece of fresh ginger, peeled and finely minced

2 garlic cloves, peeled and finely minced

8 chicken thighs

6 tbsp chilli jam

Rice and steamed greens, to serve

Preheat the oven to 220°C (425°F), Gas Mark 7. In a large dish, whisk together the rapeseed oil, soy sauce and rice wine along with the ginger and garlic.

Trim any unnecessary extra skin from the chicken thighs before adding them to the dish. Toss to coat. At this point, you can cover the dish with cling film and place in the fridge to marinate for a few hours, or you can cook them straight away.

Place the marinated chicken thighs in a large roasting tray, leaving about 2.5cm (1in) between the thighs to allow them space to crisp up. Cook for 35 minutes until crispy, then take out of the oven and use a pastry brush to brush each thigh with chilli jam until they are all coated.

Place back in the oven to cook for a further 10 minutes or until cooked all the way through. Serve with rice and steamed greens.

SQUASH & SPINACH
LENTIL CURRY

If vegetarian recipes don't get you excited, I want you to try this one – it's full of great spices and flavours and, served with rice, it's a really filling meal.

 SERVES 4–6 (V)

1 tbsp rapeseed oil

1 large onion, peeled and roughly diced

3 garlic cloves, peeled and finely chopped

1 tbsp medium curry powder, plus extra to sprinkle

1 tsp ground cumin

1 tsp coriander seeds, ground

1 tsp ground ginger

½ tsp ground cinnamon

750ml (1½ pints) vegetable stock

250g (9oz) green lentils

300g (11oz) basmati rice, well rinsed

1kg (2lb 3oz) butternut squash (about 1 squash) peeled, deseeded and chopped into 2.5cm (1in) cubes

200g (7oz) spinach

60–100g (2–3½oz) natural yoghurt

Sea salt and ground black pepper

Place a medium-sized pot over a medium–high heat and add the oil. Fry the onion and garlic for 5 minutes until softened. Add the curry powder, cumin, coriander, ginger and cinnamon and stir-fry for a further minute. Pour in the stock and add the lentils. Bring to the boil, then reduce the heat and simmer for 30 minutes.

Meanwhile, pour the rice into a cup, check the level it comes to, then pour into a cooking pot. Use the same cup to measure out twice the amount of water and pour this over the rice. Place over a medium–high heat, with the lid on, for about 15 minutes until all the water has been absorbed and the rice is cooked through. Take off the heat, fluff up with a fork and place the lid back on until you are ready to serve.

Add the cubed squash to the curry and cook for 15 minutes or until tender when pierced with a fork. Mix through the spinach until completely wilted down. The curry is now ready to serve straight away in bowls with a tablespoon of yoghurt, a sprinkle of curry powder and the warm rice.

CHEESY HAM HOCK
SPINACH CREPES

Whenever I visit Paris, one of the first things I always order is a crêpe with *jambon et fromage*. This recipe is my little twist on that – it makes vibrant green pancakes that are really nice as a brunch or lunch dish. Meat from ham hocks is a cheap and tasty alternative to prime slices of ham.

☛ SERVES 6

100g (3½oz) fresh spinach

300ml (10½fl oz) milk

150g (5oz) plain flour

2 large free-range eggs

2 tbsp melted butter

225g (8oz) Gruyère cheese, grated

260g (9oz) cooked ham hock meat (see page 42)

Put the spinach and milk in a food processor and blitz until smooth. Add the flour and eggs and blitz again to incorporate. Stir 1 tablespoon of the melted butter through the batter.

Place a frying pan over a medium–high heat and wipe with a little of the remaining melted butter. Add a ladleful of the batter and swirl the pan until the batter completely coats the base.

Cook the crêpe for 1–2 minutes on one side, then flip over, turn the heat down to low and top with a little of the cheese and ham. Cook for 1 minute before folding in half, then into quarters.

Pop the cooked crêpes into an ovenproof dish and keep warm in the oven at 120°C (225°F), Gas Mark ¼ while you repeat the process with the remaining batter, ham and cheese. Serve the crêpes straight away.

ROAST PUMPKIN
& FETA PIE

Pumpkin is one of my favourite vegetables – when they start appearing in the shops, it's a real sign that autumn has arrived. When cooking with them, try to look for ones with a really rich orange colour and that are just smaller than a football. These little pies are a great vegetarian supper when served with a little side salad.

☞ MAKES 4 PIES (V)

1 small pumpkin
(900g/2lb), peeled,
deseeded and cubed

2 tbsp olive oil

1 tsp honey

½ tsp ground cinnamon

150g (5oz) feta, crumbled

100g (3½oz) baby
spinach leaves

1 fresh thyme sprig,
leaves picked off

1 x 450g (1lb) packet of
ready-rolled puff pastry
(2 sheets)

Plain flour, for dusting

1 large free-range egg,
beaten

Sea salt and ground
black pepper

Preheat the oven to 200°C (400°F) Gas Mark 6. Place the pumpkin cubes in a large roasting tray and drizzle with oil and honey. Sprinkle with cinnamon and season with sea salt and ground black pepper. Toss to coat the pumpkin completely and place in the oven to cook for 40 minutes until tender and lightly charred.

When the pumpkin is cooked, use a potato masher to roughly mash the pumpkin in the roasting tin. Add the feta, spinach and thyme leaves and gently stir though.

Preheat the oven to 180°C (350°F), Gas Mark 4. Lay out both sheets of puff pastry on a floured work surface and cut out four 15 x 10cm (6 x 4in) and four 18 x 12cm (7 x 5in) rectangles. Dust a large baking sheet with a little flour and arrange the smaller rectangles on it.

Spoon the mashed pumpkin onto the centre of each small puff-pastry rectangle, leaving 1–2cm (½–¾in) of space around the edges. Brush the edges with some of the beaten egg and lay the larger rectangles of pastry over the top. Gently press the edges together to seal, brush with the rest of the egg and place in the oven.

Cook the little pies for 20 minutes until the pastry has puffed up and turned golden brown. Allow to cool slightly and serve straight away.

ONE-PAN-WONDER
MEXICAN EGGS

I make these eggs in the morning whenever we've had any late-night guests who decided to stay over. They make a really funky and filling brunch.

 SERVES 2–4

1 tbsp olive oil

1 red pepper, deseeded and finely chopped

1 red onion, peeled and sliced wafer-thin

1 garlic clove, peeled and finely chopped

1 x 400g (14oz) tin of chopped tomatoes

1 tsp honey

1 x 400g (14oz) tin of black-eyed beans, drained and rinsed

4 large free-range eggs

75g (2½oz) feta cheese, crumbled

Small handful of fresh coriander

1 lime, cut into wedges

Sea salt and ground black pepper

Toasted sourdough bread, to serve

Put the olive oil in a large frying pan over a high heat and fry the red pepper and half the onion for 2 minutes. Mix through the garlic and cook for a further minute.

Add the tomatoes and honey, season with sea salt and ground black pepper and allow to simmer away gently for 8 minutes until the sauce has thickened slightly. Stir through the beans until combined.

Make four wells in the tomato sauce with the back of a spoon and crack in the eggs. Sprinkle with crumbled feta cheese and a grind of black pepper. Cover the pan with a lid and cook for 6–8 minutes or until the egg whites are no longer translucent.

When cooked, garnish with fresh coriander leaves, the remaining thinly sliced red onion and lime wedges. Serve straight away with some toasted sourdough bread.

INDIAN CHICKEN & RICE BAKE

I love writing recipes that I know will become a regular part of my everyday repertoire, and this one is currently sitting in my Top Ten favourite dishes. It's an all-in-one recipe that feeds a crowd for very little. Really, the only work involved is browning the chicken legs; apart from that, the whole dish bakes in the oven while the rice soaks up all those fantastic Indian spices and flavours. Everything mingles together for a really great meal.

☛ SERVES 4–6

1-2 tbsp rapeseed oil

4-6 chicken legs (leg and thigh)

2 large onions, peeled and roughly chopped

1 tbsp medium curry powder

1 tsp each of ground cumin, coriander, turmeric and ginger

8 green cardamom pods, lightly crushed

350g (12oz) basmati rice, well rinsed

650ml (23fl oz) chicken stock

250g (9oz) frozen peas

100g (3½oz) baby spinach leaves

Sea salt and ground black pepper

Preheat the oven to 180°C (350°F), Gas Mark 4. Place a large, non-stick frying pan over a high heat, add 1 tablespoon of oil and brown the chicken legs on all sides. Remove and set aside on a plate.

Reduce the heat on the stove, add another tablespoon of oil to the pan, if required, and fry the onions until soft, for about 6 minutes. Stir in the curry powder, cumin, coriander, turmeric, ginger, cardamom pods and rice until everything is evenly combined.

Transfer the rice mix to a rectangular baking dish and place the chicken legs on top. Pour over the chicken stock and season with sea salt and ground black pepper. Cover the dish with foil and place in the oven to bake for 25 minutes.

Remove from the oven and stir the peas and spinach through the rice and around the chicken. Replace the foil and cook in the oven for a further 10 minutes until the chicken is cooked through and the rice is tender, then serve straight away.

ULTIMATE LEFTOVER
FRIED RICE

I love fried rice and you can really pump it up with healthy vegetables when you make it at home. The dish works best when you are using cooked rice from cold, so it's an ideal time to use up your leftovers instead of cooking rice from fresh. However, cold cooked rice does tend to clump together, so you need to place it in a large bowl, drizzle it with a little oil and break it up with a fork before using.

SERVES 4

1 tbsp sunflower oil

2 garlic cloves, peeled and finely grated

1 red chilli, deseeded and finely chopped

1 thumb-sized piece of fresh ginger, peeled and finely grated

Bunch of spring onions, thinly sliced

2 large carrots, peeled and thinly sliced

1 red pepper, deseeded and finely chopped

1 tsp sesame oil

1 tbsp soy sauce

1 tbsp Thai fish sauce (Nam Pla)

150g (5oz) cooked ham hock meat (see page 42), finely chopped

150g (5oz) frozen peas

300g (11oz) leftover cooked rice, cold

2 large free-range eggs, lightly whisked

Heat the sunflower oil in a large frying pan over a high heat and stir-fry the garlic, chilli and ginger for 1 minute. Add the spring onions, carrots and red pepper and stir-fry for a further 3 minutes.

Stir through the sesame oil, soy sauce and Thai fish sauce over the heat for 1 minute. Add the ham and peas and gently mix through. Add the cooked rice to the pan and mix to combine with the vegetables and ham.

Make a well in the centre and pour in the whisked eggs. Allow to set briefly, then, working quickly, stir the eggs and quickly incorporate the rice from the sides until everything is combined. Cook for 2 minutes then serve straight away in a big bowl for a quick and tasty dinner.

SIZZLING, STICKY, SPICY
MINCED PORK WITH RICE

Fried rice is one of my favourite things and I'm constantly looking for ways to mix it up. This recipe is one of my recent additions and has quickly become a regular. It is a bit of a kitchen-sink recipe, in that you can add whatever veggies you might have lying around at the bottom of the fridge, so feel free to experiment. Whenever I'm cooking rice for dinner, I always make a little more than I need, specifically so that I have leftovers to use in recipes like this. When storing leftover cooked rice, place it in an unsealed airtight container and pop it in a cool place to cool quickly and completely, before sealing and transferring to the fridge. Only reheat previously cooked rice once.

SERVES 4

1 tbsp sunflower oil

250g (9oz) pork mince

1 red chilli, deseeded and finely chopped

1 thumb-sized piece of fresh ginger, peeled and finely minced

1 tbsp dark soy sauce

1 tbsp oyster sauce

2 tsp caster sugar

300g (11oz) leftover cooked rice, cold

200g (7oz) sugar snap peas, finely sliced

Bunch of spring onions, finely sliced

2 large free-range eggs, beaten

1 mint sprig, leaves finely sliced

1 lime, cut into wedges, to garnish (optional)

Place a large frying pan or wok over a high heat and add the oil. Fry the pork quickly, using a large wooden spatula to break up the meat until it becomes fine and any liquid has cooked out.

Add the chilli, ginger, soy sauce, oyster sauce and sugar and stir-fry for 2 minutes. Add the cooked rice, sugar snap peas and most of the spring onions, and stir-fry for a further minute or until the vegetables are just slightly tender.

Make a well in the centre of the wok and pour in the beaten eggs. Allow to set partially before mixing through the rice. Mix in most of the mint and serve in deep bowls with an extra sprinkle of spring onions and mint and a wedge of lime, if you like.

STEAMED ASIAN MACKEREL PARCELS

These little parcels certainly know how to make an entrance. When you serve them, make sure you get your guests to open the parcels themselves, to reveal the steaming mackerel inside. You can use this method with any fish; it's nice served with a little rice.

SERVES 4

1 large thumb-sized piece of fresh ginger, peeled and finely minced

2 garlic cloves, peeled and finely minced

1 tbsp rice wine

2 tbsp light soy sauce

1 tsp sesame oil

4 baby bok choy, shredded

4 mackerel fillets, pin-boned

6 spring onions, finely sliced

1 red chilli, deseeded and finely sliced

Preheat the oven to 200°C (400°F), Gas Mark 6. Cut out four sheets of parchment paper, each twice the size of a mackerel fillet. Whisk together the ginger, garlic, rice wine, soy sauce and sesame oil.

Arrange the bok choy on the parchment sheets and top each with a mackerel fillet, some spring onion and chilli. Spoon the garlic and rice wine mixture over each fillet. Fold up the sides of the parchment paper and seal the corners with metal paper clips.

Place on a baking tray and cook in the oven for about 10 minutes until the mackerel is cooked and the bok choy is tender. Serve straight to the table, allowing your guests to tear open the paper to reveal the steaming mackerel.

THAI RED
FISH CURRY

I love the zingy flavours of this curry. Fish such as haddock and whiting are affordable and can all be used here, so try them instead of cod – just ask your fishmonger to remove the skin and bones. You could also quite easily use chicken instead of fish, though bear in mind that it would require a longer cooking time. I have suggested adding sugar snap peas and baby corn but you could add sliced peppers, sweet potato or peas, if you wish.

 SERVES 4

250g (9oz) basmati rice,
well rinsed

1 tbsp rapeseed oil

2 shallots, peeled and
finely sliced

3 tbsp Thai red curry paste

400ml (14fl oz) coconut milk

200ml (7fl oz)
vegetable stock

Juice of 2 limes

1 tbsp Thai fish sauce
(Nam Pla)

1 tsp brown sugar

150g (5oz) sugar snap peas

100g (3½oz) baby corn,
sliced lengthways

3–4 fish fillets (600g/1lb
5oz in total), cut into
2.5cm (1in) cubes

Good handful of basil
and coriander leaves

Pour the rice into a cup, check the level it comes to, then pour into a cooking pot. Use the same cup to measure out twice the amount of water and pour this over the rice. Place over a medium–high heat with the lid on for about 15 minutes until all the water has been absorbed and the rice is cooked through. Take off the heat, fluff up with a fork and place the lid back on until you are ready to serve.

While the rice is cooking, heat the oil in a separate cooking pot over a medium–high heat and add the shallots. Fry for 3–4 minutes until softened. Add the red curry paste and fry for a further minute or so, stirring to coat the shallots.

Pour in the coconut milk and vegetable stock and bring to a steady boil, simmering for 8–10 minutes. Add the lime juice, fish sauce and brown sugar. Stir in the sugar snap peas and baby corn and simmer for 3 minutes.

Add in the fish pieces and simmer for 3–5 minutes until just cooked. Stir through some of the basil and coriander leaves before serving the curry in bowls over rice. Garnish with the last few basil and coriander leaves.

FRIDGE LEFTOVERS
FRITTATA

Even the most sorry-looking kitchens should have a few eggs, veggies and a bit of leftover cheese knocking around. My fridge leftovers frittata is a great little lunchtime dish; it's a filling base for lots of additions, depending on what's in your kitchen. Try adding leftover ham, chorizo, spinach, peas, herbs – all sorts, really.

☞ SERVES 4 (V)

1 tbsp rapeseed oil

1 red onion, peeled and finely sliced

½ courgette, chopped into 1cm (½in) slices

2 red or yellow peppers, deseeded and sliced

1 garlic clove, peeled and finely chopped

8 large free-range eggs

Generous knob of butter

75g (2½oz) cheese (Gruyère, Cheddar or Parmesan)

Sea salt and ground black pepper

Salad leaves, to serve

Place a large, non-stick frying pan with an ovenproof (metal) handle over a high heat, add the oil and fry the onion, courgette and peppers until tender. Add the garlic and fry for a further 1 minute.

Whisk the eggs in a large bowl until just combined, then add the contents of the frying pan and gently mix through until coated. Season with sea salt and ground black pepper.

Place the frying pan back over a medium–high heat and add the butter, melting it until it foams. Pour the egg and vegetable mixture into the pan and evenly distribute the vegetables. Sprinkle over the cheese.

Cook for 4 minutes until the bottom of the frittata is golden brown, then place the pan under a hot grill to puff up for a further 3–4 minutes until golden on top.

Remove the frittata from the pan and cut into quarters on a chopping board. Serve with a little side salad for a quick and tasty lunch or dinner.

CHILLI HONEY-GLAZED
PORK CHOPS

My girlfriend Sofie is obsessed with pork chops; don't ask me why, but it's always the first thing she requests when I ask what she wants for dinner. Not that I'm complaining, though, as they are quick to prepare and cook, and they make a simple dinner when served with greens and a little cooked rice. This recipe has a lovely Asian twist.

 SERVES 4

3 tbsp honey

1 tbsp hoisin sauce

1 garlic clove, peeled and finely minced

1 red chilli, deseeded and finely sliced

½ tsp ground star anise

Grated zest of 1 orange and juice of ½

4 medium-sized pork chops (approx. 600g/1lb 5oz)

Wilted spinach and rice, to serve

In a bowl, whisk together the honey, hoisin, garlic, chilli, star anise, orange zest and juice. Toss the chops in the bowl and leave for 15 minutes, or cover and place in the fridge to marinate preferably overnight.

When ready to cook, place the chops on a large grill tray lined with foil. (It's worth covering your tray with foil to save scrubbing off the sticky mixture later on.) Cook under a hot grill for 6 minutes on each side, until crispy and cooked through.

Serve alongside some wilted spinach and rice for a delicious and zesty supper.

CRISPY MUSTARD CHICKEN TRAY BAKE

All-in-one recipes always bring a smile to my face, and this one is a real family-pleaser. You could use any other veggies you want here but I do like this combination of tomatoes and sweet potato. Use a big roasting tray as you need to allow space for all the ingredients, otherwise they won't roast up and become crispy.

SERVES 4

3 tbsp Dijon mustard

2 garlic cloves, peeled and finely chopped

1 tsp honey

8 tbsp breadcrumbs

2 fresh thyme sprigs, leaves stripped

8 free-range chicken thighs

2 sweet potatoes, peeled and chopped into chunks

1 punnet of cherry tomatoes, sliced in half

2 tbsp rapeseed oil

Sea salt and ground black pepper

Preheat the oven to 220°C (425°F), Gas Mark 7. In a small bowl, mix together the mustard, garlic and honey. Season with sea salt and ground black pepper. In another bowl, mix together the breadcrumbs with the thyme leaves.

Trim off any extra pieces of fat or skin from the chicken thighs. Arrange the thighs in a large, high-sided roasting tin and spread about a dessertspoonful of the mustard mixture over the flesh of each until coated. Sprinkle each thigh with the breadcrumb mixture and gently press it down.

Arrange the sweet potato chunks and tomatoes around the chicken, allowing plenty of space between the ingredients so that they roast rather than stew, then drizzle with the oil. Season with sea salt and ground black pepper.

Place in the oven to cook for 40–45 minutes, basting with the cooking juices halfway through the time. Cook until the chicken is done all the way through and the sweet potato is tender when pierced with a fork. Cover the dish with foil if the tops begin to char.

Serve the crispy chicken thighs straight away with the tomatoes and sweet potato chunks on the side.

BAKED POTATO
FEAST

For the perfect baked potato, run it under water and then sprinkle with sea salt. This helps the skin to dry out and become crispy. Place in a hot oven at 200°C (400°F), Gas Mark 6, straight onto the wire rack, and bake for 45 minutes or until tender when pierced with a fork. When ready, slice open and you have the most perfect vehicle for lots of different toppings and flavours. Try these ideas for quick, cheap suppers...

☞ EACH MAKES
ENOUGH FOR
2 BAKED POTATOES

Baked Beans and Cheese (V)
A student favourite, which needs no excuses. Simply top potatoes with hot baked beans and sprinkle with freshly grated Cheddar cheese. Dig in straight away.

Chilli Con Carne
This spicy, meaty addition makes the perfect topping for a baked potato. I use leftovers from my Slow-cooked Meaty Chilli (see page 39), which I reheat and spoon over the freshly baked potatoes. Serve with a generous spoonful of crème fraîche.

Smoked Mackerel and Dijon Mustard
Think mini fish pie! This is a wonderful combination of flavours that really work well together. Simply scoop out the flesh from the baked potatoes, pop the skins on a baking sheet and back into the oven to crisp up. Mash the potato flesh with some shop-bought or home-smoked (see page 98) mackerel, a little single cream and a teaspoon or two of Dijon mustard. Season with sea salt and ground black pepper, then scoop back into the potato skins, sprinkle with a little Cheddar cheese and place under a hot grill until the tops turn golden.

Tomato and Smoked Streaky Bacon
Another lovely way to serve baked potatoes: tear open freshly baked potatoes on a baking tray, mash them down a little with the back of a fork and top with a basic tomato sauce (see page 112), some crispy smoked streaky bacon and a sprinkle of grated cheese. Place in the oven at 200°C (400°F), Gas Mark 6 until the cheese has melted.

TURKEY MEATLOAF WITH A
SPICY BEAN SAUCE

Meatloaf is true, unashamed comfort food and should be celebrated for being just that. You can make one big meatloaf and serve it in slices or make mini ones and serve each sitting proudly on top of the spicy bean stew.

 SERVES 4–6

Butter, for greasing

450g (1lb) turkey mince

2 garlic cloves, peeled and finely minced

1 medium onion, peeled and finely chopped

1 celery stalk, trimmed and finely chopped

1 green pepper, deseeded and finely chopped

2 slices of white bread, whizzed in a food processor

1 egg, lightly beaten

1 tsp Tabasco sauce

5 tbsp tomato ketchup

Sea salt and ground black pepper

For the spicy bean stew

1 tbsp rapeseed oil

1 medium onion, peeled and sliced into half-moons

1 red and 1 yellow pepper, deseeded and finely sliced

1 tsp ground cumin

1 tsp dried oregano

1 tsp sugar

2 x 400g (14oz) tins of chopped tomatoes

1 x 400g (14oz) tin of cannellini beans, drained and rinsed

Preheat the oven to 200°C (400°F), Gas Mark 6. Grease a 900g (2lb) loaf tin.

In a large bowl, use a spoon to mix together the turkey, garlic, onion, celery, green pepper, breadcrumbs, egg, Tabasco sauce, 1 tablespoon of the ketchup and a pinch of sea salt and ground black pepper.

Press the mixture into the loaf tin and spread the remaining tomato ketchup over the top. Place in the oven to cook for 40–45 minutes. The meat will come away slightly from the sides of the tin and the ketchup will lightly char.

While the meatloaf is cooking, make the spicy bean stew. Place a large frying pan over a high heat, add the oil and fry the onion and peppers quickly for 2 minutes. Reduce the heat to medium–low and continue to cook until the contents of the pan have become soft. Stir through the cumin, oregano and sugar and cook for a further 5 minutes.

Stir through the tomatoes, season with sea salt and ground black pepper and simmer for 10 minutes. Stir through the beans and cook for a further 3–5 minutes. Serve the stew on deep plates with slices of meatloaf in the middle.

EVERYDAY EASY

SUPPERS

BAKING

PASTA

SIMPLE

SIDES

☞ CHEAP &

HEALTHY

SLOW-COOKED MEALS

DESSERTS

SOUPS & STEWS

Nº3

Eating healthily is not all about superfoods and expensive fad diets. It can actually be quite cost-effective and still makes use of basic, good, home-cooking skills. In my opinion, if you can learn to cook at home you are already on the right track to healthy eating, and by including just a few key ingredients in your everyday diet you will soon feel on top of the world!

From before I was born, my parents have run a business based around fruit and vegetables, so there was always a great emphasis on fresh produce when I was growing up. We were encouraged to try new things and my mom was on a constant mission to get us eating our greens.

However, despite mom's efforts with all the family, my dad has always been a bit of a 'meat and two veg' kind of guy. While he'll eat lots of traditional vegetables, he will turn his nose up at certain ingredients, such as bulgur wheat and lentils. Now that I understand the importance of including a variety of healthy ingredients into my diet, I'm permanently trying to get him to try different foods in some of my recipes. Over the last few years I've finally been able to twist his arm a little and now he's beginning to eat all sorts of different healthy ingredients. I never thought I would see him trying the types of meals in this chapter, but if they're presented nicely and taste good, you can just about win anyone over!

The beautiful thing is that some of the cheapest ingredients – veggies, mackerel and storecupboard essentials such as lentils, bulgur wheat and pearl barley – are all highly nutritious and incredibly easy to include in your diet. I believe that healthy food should be exciting to eat, so I hope that the recipes here will inspire you to include more of the good stuff in your diet and will hopefully prove that it isn't too difficult to do just that, while also creating delicious meals.

SWEET POTATO CAKES

Sweet potatoes are a great vehicle for lots of different flavours. These little sweet potato cakes can take the heat of the chilli and the creamy saltiness of the feta. They go wonderfully with a salad and sweet chilli dressing for a light lunch, or as part of a breakfast with bacon and eggs.

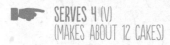

SERVES 4 (V)
(MAKES ABOUT 12 CAKES)

2 large free-range eggs

150g (5oz) plain flour

100ml (3½fl oz) milk

400g (14oz) peeled and grated sweet potatoes (about 2 medium-sized)

5 spring onions, finely chopped

75g (2½oz) feta cheese, crumbled

1 red chilli, deseeded and finely chopped

Sunflower oil, for frying

Sea salt and ground black pepper

Dressed salad leaves, to serve

In a large bowl, whisk together the eggs, flour and milk. Add in the grated sweet potato, most of the spring onion (save a little to use as a garnish), feta cheese and red chilli. Season with sea salt and ground black pepper, though be sparing with the salt as the feta cheese can itself be quite salty. Using a wooden spoon, mix until everything is evenly combined.

Pour about 1cm (½in) of oil into a large, non-stick frying pan and place over a medium–high heat. Place four separate heaped tablespoons of the sweet potato mixture into the pan and flatten each little patty with the back of the spoon. Fry for about 3–4 minutes on each side, or until golden brown. You will need a good spatula to turn them over.

Sprinkle the reserved spring onion on top and serve alongside a handful of dressed salad leaves for a delicious little lunch.

ROAST BEETROOT, FETA &
LENTIL SALAD

There are a few vegetables I can grow without fail and thankfully one of them is the mighty beetroot, which roasts beautifully and is a great addition to this lentil salad. This dish is nice at lunchtime and is excellent in lunchboxes.

☛ SERVES 4 (V)

400g (14oz) beetroot

2 tbsp rapeseed oil

300g (11oz) green lentils

150g (5oz) feta cheese

1 small red onion, peeled and finely sliced

Handful each of flat-leaf parsley, chives and dill, roughly chopped

For the dressing

3 tbsp extra-virgin olive oil

1 tbsp white wine vinegar

1 garlic clove, peeled and finely minced

1 tsp Dijon mustard

Sea salt and ground black pepper

Preheat the oven to 200°C (400°F), Gas Mark 6. Trim any leaves and stalks from the beetroot and place in a roasting tin. Toss with the oil, then wrap the whole tin with foil and place in the oven to roast for about 45 minutes or so, depending on the size of the beetroot. When ready, the beetroot should be tender when pierced with a fork.

Remove the beetroot from the oven and allow to cool before removing the skin with your fingers or a paring knife. Slice the flesh into bite-sized pieces.

In a large bowl, whisk together the ingredients for the dressing and season with the sea salt and ground black pepper.

Place the lentils in a small cooking pot and fill up with water, place over a high heat and bring to the boil. Reduce the heat and simmer for 20 minutes until tender. Drain and rinse under cold water, then add the lentils to the bowl with the dressing.

Add to the bowl the roasted beets, feta, red onion and chopped herbs and toss to combine. Serve straight away on a large serving platter for people to help themselves.

SALAD OF SARDINES,
ROASTED TOMATO & CRISPY BREADCRUMBS

The combination of sardines with slow-roasted tomatoes from the late-summer glut is one of my favourite sunshine meals.

 SERVES 4

250g (9oz) cherry tomatoes, sliced in half

450g (1lb) plum tomatoes, sliced in half

Good-quality extra-virgin olive oil, to drizzle

1 tbsp balsamic vinegar

Handful of chopped fresh herbs or 1 tsp dried oregano

2 tbsp rapeseed oil

2 garlic cloves, peeled and finely sliced

1 red chilli, deseeded and finely chopped

1 rosemary sprig

100g (3½oz) breadcrumbs

8 sardines

Juice of 1 lemon

Sea salt and ground black pepper

Preheat the oven to 180°C (350°F), Gas Mark 4. Arrange the tomatoes in a large roasting tray, cut-side up, and drizzle with olive oil and the balsamic vinegar. Sprinkle over any chopped herbs from the garden, or the oregano, and season with sea salt and ground black pepper. Place in the oven to cook for 50 minutes until reduced and caramelised.

While the tomatoes are cooking, place a large frying pan over a medium–high heat and add 1 tablespoon of the rapeseed oil. Fry the garlic, chilli and rosemary sprig for 1 minute before adding the breadcrumbs. Cook for about 5 minutes or until the breadcrumbs are crisp and golden. Transfer to a plate and discard the rosemary.

Heat the remaining tablespoon of rapeseed oil in the pan over a medium–high heat and season the sardines with sea salt and black pepper before frying for 3–4 minutes on either side, squeezing with lemon juice halfway through the cooking time.

Serve straight away on a big platter along with the tomatoes and sprinkled with the spicy breadcrumbs.

ROAST SWEET POTATOES
WITH SPICED YOGHURT & HERBS

Simply roasted sweet potatoes are a thing of beauty, and make a nice lunch or light supper topped with spiced yoghurt, sliced chilli and coriander. True healthy comfort food, if such a thing exists!

☛ SERVES 4 (V)

4 large sweet potatoes

1 tbsp rapeseed oil

150g (5oz) natural yoghurt

1 tsp ground cumin

1 tsp paprika

1 garlic clove, peeled and finely minced

1 red chilli, deseeded if you wish and finely sliced diagonally

Good handful of coriander leaves

Preheat the oven to 200°C (400°F), Gas Mark 6. Place the potatoes on a baking tray and drizzle with a little oil. Bake in the oven for 45 minutes or until tender when pierced with a fork.

Remove the potatoes from the baking tray and slice open to reveal the flesh. Place on serving plates.

Mix the yoghurt with the spices and garlic and spoon a generous dollop onto each sweet potato. Sprinkle over the red chilli and roughly tear over some coriander leaves.

AUBERGINE
LASAGNE

Aubergine Parmigiana is one of my most favourite dishes and it gave me the inspiration for this lasagne. Although it doesn't completely cut out the fat content of a regular lasagne, layering it with aubergine is certainly healthier than using pasta. It's also veggie-friendly (as long as you use vegetarian cheese instead of Parmesan) but I don't think any meat-eater would turn their nose up at this.

 SERVES 6–8 (V)
(if vegetarian cheese is used)

3–4 large aubergines, sliced lengthways, roughly 1cm (½in) in thickness
4 tbsp rapeseed oil
Butter, for greasing
50g (2oz) Parmesan cheese, grated
Sea salt and ground black pepper

For the tomato sauce
1 tbsp rapeseed oil
1 large onion, peeled and finely chopped
2 garlic cloves, peeled and finely chopped
1 tsp chilli flakes
1 tsp dried oregano
2 x 400g (14oz) tins of chopped tomatoes
1 tsp sugar

For the white sauce
75g (2½oz) butter, cut into cubes
75g (2½oz) plain flour
500ml (18fl oz) milk
Pinch of grated nutmeg

Begin with the tomato sauce. Heat the oil in a large frying pan over a medium–high heat and fry the onion for 3–4 minutes until softened. Add the garlic, chilli flakes and oregano and fry for a further 2 minutes, stirring every now and then. Add the tomatoes and sugar and season with a little sea salt and ground black pepper. Bring to the boil, then reduce the heat and continue to cook at a steady simmer for 15 minutes or until the sauce has reduced and thickened.

While the tomato sauce is cooking, lay the aubergine slices out on a large grill tray and brush both sides with oil. Do this in batches if they won't all fit. Season with sea salt and ground black pepper, then place under a hot grill to soften and lightly colour. Set aside on a plate.

Prepare the white sauce by putting the butter, flour and milk in a saucepan over a medium heat and whisking continuously until the ingredients come together and the sauce will just hold a figure of eight when swirled with the whisk. Stir in the nutmeg and remove from the heat.

Preheat the oven to 200°C (400°F), Gas Mark 6. Grease a large Pyrex or ovenproof dish, approximately 30 x 20 x 5cm (12 x 8 x 2in), and pour half the tomato sauce over the base. Top this with half the white sauce and then a layer of the grilled aubergine slices. Repeat this process, finishing with white sauce on top. Sprinkle with grated Parmesan cheese and place in the oven to bake for 25–30 minutes until golden brown on top. Remove from the oven and allow to sit for a few minutes before serving in generous portions.

STUFFED
CABBAGE ROLLS

One of the first times I cooked on TV, I went along to the studio before the big day to watch Lorraine Fitzmaurice – who owns Blazing Salads, a fantastic deli in Dublin – cook stuffed cabbage rolls. I hadn't had my lunch, so once the show was over I joined the crew in the scramble to get my hands on some of the leftovers. Here's my take on this surprisingly tasty vegetarian dish.

 SERVES 4–6 (V)

1 Savoy cabbage

1 tbsp olive oil

1 large onion, peeled and finely chopped

2 large garlic cloves, peeled and finely chopped

250g (9oz) mushrooms, finely chopped

Small bunch of parsley, finely chopped

1 tsp thyme leaves

75g (2½oz) goat's cheese, crumbled

50g (2oz) walnuts, toasted and roughly chopped

300g (11oz) cooked bulgur wheat (100g/3½oz uncooked)

Sea salt and ground black pepper

For the tomato sauce

1 tbsp olive oil

1 onion, peeled and finely chopped

2 x 400g (14oz) tins of chopped tomatoes

1 tbsp honey

1 tbsp balsamic vinegar

Place a large cooking pot of water over a high heat and bring to the boil. Remove the tougher outer leaves of the cabbage and discard. Gently break away the inner leaves and place them in the boiling water for 5 minutes or until tender.

Plunge the blanched leaves into a sink of cold water to stop them cooking further. Drain and pat dry with a clean tea towel.

Put the oil in a large, non-stick frying pan over a medium–high heat, add the onion and garlic and fry for 4 minutes. Add the chopped mushrooms and season with sea salt and ground black pepper, frying for a further 3–4 minutes. Mix through the parsley, thyme, goat's cheese, walnuts and bulgur wheat. Remove the filling from the pan and set aside on a plate.

For the tomato sauce, place the olive oil in the frying pan and fry the onion over a medium–high heat for 6 minutes until soft. Add the tomatoes, and fill one of the tins up with water and add this too. Season with sea salt and ground black pepper and mix through with the honey and balsamic vinegar. Bring to a steady simmer and cook for 15 minutes.

While the tomato sauce is simmering, preheat the oven to 180°C (350°F), Gas Mark 4. To fill and roll the cabbage leaves, place 2 tablespoons of the filling onto each leaf, fold both sides in and roll up. Be careful not to roll the parcels too tightly.

Place half the tomato sauce in the base of a baking dish. Place all the cabbage rolls on top and finally cover with the remaining tomato sauce. Cover with foil and bake for 45 minutes.

CHEAT'S HOME-HOT-SMOKED
MACKEREL SALAD

My dad is a bit of a culinary 'Rain Man'. You wouldn't think he had it in him, but then he pulls out true inspiration like this. He is essentially responsible for the addition of this genius little method to my life, which makes hot-smoked mackerel in a few easy steps. He came up with it in an attempt to use up a glut of mackerel during one summer and we've been making it ever since. The mackerel goes really well in this zingy salad, but can also be used in pasta or whizzed up into a smoked mackerel pâté. For the smoking, you will need woodchips, 12–16 wooden skewers, 8 aluminium takeaway boxes and kitchen foil.

SERVES 4

700g (1½lb) baby potatoes

4 rosemary sprigs

4 thyme sprigs

4 mackerel fillets, pin-boned

1 tbsp extra-virgin olive oil

Juice of 1 lemon

100ml (3½fl oz) crème fraîche

200g (7oz) mixed salad leaves

Sea salt and ground black pepper

Place the potatoes in a cooking pot of water, bring to the boil and cook for 15 minutes or until the potatoes are tender when pierced with a fork. Drain and set aside to cool, before slicing in half.

Prepare the mini smokers by popping a handful of woodchips and a sprig each of rosemary and thyme into four aluminium takeaway boxes. Push 3–4 skewers across the top of each box.

Place the mackerel fillets on a plate and generously season on both sides with sea salt and ground black pepper. Arrange each mackerel fillet skin-side down on top of the skewers on each box. Place the remaining aluminium boxes on top and wrap them all in foil. Put the wrapped boxes over a hot barbecue, cover with a lid and allow to smoke for 15 minutes.

Remove the mackerel from the homemade smokers, allow to cool, then remove the flesh and flake with a fork. Set aside on a plate.

Whisk together the oil, lemon juice and crème fraîche in a small bowl. Arrange the salad leaves on a large serving platter, place the potatoes on top and scatter with the smoked mackerel. Drizzle with the creamy dressing and serve straight away.

ROAST SQUASH & BULGUR WHEAT SALAD

Bulgur wheat is an excellent grain to keep in the storecupboard. It's easy to prepare and quite healthy too, and is made in the same way that you cook couscous. This is a tasty vegetarian salad, which can be eaten warm or cold, and makes a filling lunchbox dish. You can also add some toasted nuts or some seeds for extra crunch.

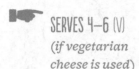

SERVES 4–6 (V)

(if vegetarian cheese is used)

1kg (2lb 3oz) butternut squash, peeled, deseeded and chopped into 2.5cm (1in) chunks

1–2 tbsp rapeseed oil

½ tsp ground cinnamon

250g (9oz) bulgur wheat

3 tbsp extra-virgin olive oil

1 tbsp cider vinegar

1 tsp honey

100g (3½ oz) blue cheese, crumbled

75g (2 ½ oz) rocket, roughly chopped

Sea salt and ground black pepper

Preheat the oven to 200°C (400°F), Gas Mark 6. In a roasting tin, toss the butternut squash with the rapeseed oil. Sprinkle with cinnamon and a generous seasoning of sea salt and ground black pepper. Place in the oven to cook for 40–45 minutes until tender and slightly charred on the edges. Remove from the oven and allow to cool.

Measure the bulgur wheat into a cup, check the level it comes to, then pour into a bowl. Fill the cup with the same amount of boiling water and add to the bowl. Cover with cling film and allow the bulgur wheat to soak up all the liquid.

In a small bowl, whisk together the olive oil, cider vinegar and honey. Season with sea salt and ground black pepper.

When the bulgur wheat is ready, use a fork to fluff it up. Add in the roasted squash, crumbled cheese, rocket and dressing and toss gently to combine. Serve straight away or cover with cling film and place in the fridge.

ZINGY TINNED-PULSE
SUPER SALAD

Need a quick salad in next to no time? Here's your answer – it's cheap, tasty and uses mostly storecupboard ingredients.

 SERVES 4–6 (V)

1 red pepper

3 tbsp extra-virgin olive oil

1 tbsp red wine vinegar

1 tsp Dijon mustard

1 x 400g (14oz) tin each of cannellini beans, kidney beans and chickpeas, drained and rinsed

150g (5oz) tin of sweetcorn, drained and rinsed

1 red onion, peeled and finely sliced

Small handful of freshly chopped flat-leaf parsley

Sea salt and ground black pepper

Preheat the oven to 220°C (425°F), Gas Mark 7. Roast the red pepper in the hot oven for 30 minutes until the skin is blackened and blistered. Pop into a zip-lock food bag and leave until cool, then remove the skin and seeds and slice into strips.

In a large bowl, whisk together the olive oil, red wine vinegar, Dijon mustard, sea salt and ground black pepper. Taste, and make any adjustments as necessary.

Add the cannellini and kidney beans, chickpeas, sweetcorn, red onion slices and red pepper strips to the bowl and toss to combine.

Just before you serve, stir through the freshly chopped parsley. Serve straight away or cover in cling film and pop in the fridge until you are ready to serve.

MOROCCAN
CHICKPEA BURGERS

Decent burgers from storecupboard ingredients, who'd have thought? I love these little Moroccan veggie burgers – they have a great, nutty flavour.

 SERVES 4 (V)

1 x 400g (14oz) tin of chickpeas, drained and rinsed

60g (2oz) breadcrumbs

2 tbsp tahini paste or smooth peanut butter

1 large free-range egg

1 tsp ground coriander

1 tsp ground cumin

6 spring onions, chopped

2 tbsp rapeseed oil

150g (5oz) natural yoghurt

1 tsp garam masala

Sea salt and ground black pepper

Wholegrain pitta breads, salad leaves and grated carrot, to serve

Place half the chickpeas in a food processor with the breadcrumbs, tahini paste, egg, coriander and cumin and blitz until smooth. Remove the blade and stir through the remaining chickpeas and the spring onions. Season with sea salt and ground black pepper.

Form the mixture into four 10cm (4in) burgers by hand or using a burger press. Place on a plate and cover, leaving to sit in the fridge for at least 2 hours to firm up.

Place a large frying pan over a medium–high heat and add the oil. Fry the burgers in the pan for 5–6 minutes on each side, until they have a nice golden colour.

In a small bowl, mix the yoghurt with the garam masala. Toast and split some wholegrain pitta breads. Serve the warm burgers in the pitta breads with the spiced yoghurt, salad leaves and grated carrot.

PEARL BARLEY
RISOTTO

My love for pearl barley increased the minute I used it in a risotto. This is a basic recipe, to which, just like a regular risotto, you can add lots of extra flavours to bring out its true beauty. Try it with steamed asparagus and peas, pan-fried garlic mushrooms, and roasted squash and pancetta.

☛ SERVES 4 (V)
(if vegetable stock & vegetarian cheese is used)

50g (2oz) butter

1 large onion, peeled and finely chopped

2 garlic cloves, peeled and finely chopped

300g (11oz) pearl barley

1.5 litres (2½ pints) vegetable or chicken stock

75g (2½oz) Parmesan cheese, finely grated

Sea salt and ground black pepper

Place a large frying pan over a medium–high heat and add half the butter. When the butter has melted and started to foam, add in the onion and garlic and fry gently for 6–8 minutes. Add the pearl barley and stir it through for 2 minutes.

Pour in half the stock and bring to the boil, then simmer for about 20 minutes, adding more stock as required and stirring the grains very frequently.

When all the liquid has been absorbed and the pearl barley is tender, take the pan off the heat and stir through the remaining butter and the grated Parmesan. At this point you could also stir through any extra ingredients or flavours of your choice.

Season with sea salt and ground black pepper and serve.

SUPERFOOD STIR-FRY

Stir-fries are quick, versatile and healthy and I particularly like how you can take your time prepping all the ingredients but the cooking all takes place in just a few fast and sizzling minutes!

 SERVES 4 (V)

2 tbsp sunflower or groundnut oil

2 garlic cloves, peeled and finely chopped

1 thumb-sized piece of fresh ginger, peeled and finely grated

1 red chilli, deseeded and finely chopped

2 red onions, peeled and finely sliced

2 red peppers, deseeded and finely sliced

1 broccoli, broken into florets and finely sliced

Juice of 1 lime

1 tbsp soy sauce

1 tsp sesame oil

Generous handful of salted peanuts, roughly chopped

Heat the oil in a large wok over a high heat until just before it begins to smoke, then add the garlic, ginger and chilli. Stir-fry for about 30 seconds before adding the onions and cooking for 3 minutes.

Add the peppers and broccoli to the wok and stir-fry for 6–8 minutes until just tender, stirring frequently. Halfway through the cooking time, mix in the lime juice, soy sauce and sesame oil.

Serve from the wok at the table with a generous sprinkling of chopped salted peanuts.

EVERYDAY EASY SUPPERS

BAKING

PASTA

SIMPLE SIDES

CHEAP & HEALTHY

SLOW-COOKED MEALS

SOUPS & STEWS

DESSERTS

Up until the age of seven, I refused point-blank to even try pasta – in my mind it was a hot pile of rubbery blandness that had no real importance to any of the types of food I liked. That all changed on a trip to Italy, when in a restaurant I was served a huge bowl of rich and sweet tomatoey spaghetti, which I watched a typically Italian waiter dust from a height with Parmesan cheese. I reluctantly tucked in but after one sucked, slurped and savoured mouthful I knew that this staple Italian ingredient was for me.

When we came home, I insisted my aunt Erica show me how to make the fresh stuff and so we spent an afternoon together, with a rickety old pasta-rolling machine clamped to the kitchen table, covered in flour as we made up thin yellow sheets of pasta. While they dried off, draped over the handle of a broom propped across two chairs, we set about making a spicy tomato sauce. The fresh pasta was then plunged into boiling water and a few minutes later drained straight from the water with tongs, before being plonked and mingled into the big pan of sauce and served in generous portions. Heaven in a bowl!

Fresh pasta is incredibly inexpensive to make, but as a nation, for convenience purposes, we have adopted the dried variety as one of our staple storecupboard ingredients. Although quite different from its fresh cousin, dried pasta is just as delicious and makes a filling and cheap base for lots of fantastic dishes. It's generally just a bit of an all-rounder and I love the fact that after it's spent less than 15 minutes in the pot, I have the bones of a great dinner underway with very little fuss. These pasta dishes are all total bargains, in that they will feed a crowd using simple ingredients, healthy vegetables and inexpensive cuts of meat.

SAUSAGE MEAT & CHICKEN LIVER RAGU

This is a rich and flavourful twist on a traditional ragù sauce. Both sausage meat and chicken livers are inexpensive to buy and combined they make a wonderful base for this sauce, which is ideal with pasta.

 SERVES 4

1 tbsp rapeseed oil

1 onion, peeled and finely chopped

2 garlic cloves, peeled and finely chopped

350g (12oz) sausage meat

150g (5oz) chicken livers, well trimmed and finely chopped

1 x 400g (14oz) tin of chopped tomatoes

½ glass of white wine (about 150ml/5fl oz)

½ tsp freshly chopped thyme

300g (11oz) rigatoni pasta

1 tbsp crème fraîche

Sea salt and ground black pepper

Parmesan shavings, to serve, (optional)

Place a medium frying pan over a medium–high heat, add 1 tablespoon of oil and fry the onion and garlic for 5 minutes until softened. Remove from the pan and set aside on a plate.

Fry the sausage meat, breaking it up with a wooden spoon until it browns. Add the chicken livers and cook for a further 3 minutes.

Return the onion and garlic to the pan, stir in the tomatoes, white wine and thyme and bring to a steady simmer. Cook for 15 minutes until the sauce has reduced.

Place a large cooking pot of water over a high heat and bring to the boil. Cook the pasta until al dente.

Remove the frying pan from the heat, stir the crème fraîche through the ragù, and season with sea salt and ground black pepper to taste. Drain the pasta, then return it to its pot and fold in the ragù. Sprinkle over Parmesan shavings, if you like, to serve.

CAULIFLOWER & BROCCOLI
MAC 'N' CHEESE

At one of my recent cookery demonstrations I got a great tip to make an all-in-one white sauce, which simplifies the process here. There are two things that are key to this method: the milk must be cold when you start, and remember to keep whisking vigorously until the sauce thickens. If you want to take this simple recipe one step further, add some fried smoked streaky bacon bits. This is a great dish for a leftovers lunchbox the next day.

 **SERVES 4–6 (V)**

250g (9oz) macaroni

1 cauliflower, broken into florets

1 broccoli, broken into florets

700ml (1¼ pints) cold milk

50g (2oz) butter, plus extra for greasing

50g (2oz) plain flour

1 tsp wholegrain mustard

Pinch of nutmeg

200g (7oz) Cheddar cheese, grated

Sea salt and ground black pepper

Fill a large cooking pot (big enough to hold the cooked pasta, broccoli and cauliflower) with water and bring to the boil over a high heat. Add the macaroni and cook until al dente, for about 12 minutes.

Five minutes before the pasta is cooked, add the cauliflower florets to the water. Two minutes later, add the broccoli florets. (If you don't have enough space, just put on a second pot of boiling water.) Cook for the remaining 3 minutes, then drain the whole lot, place back in the pot and set aside.

Preheat the oven to 200°C (400°F), Gas Mark 6. Grease a 25cm (10in) square, ovenproof baking dish, approximately 5cm (2in) in depth.

Add the milk to a saucepan over a medium–high heat and then whisk in the butter and flour. Continuously whisk until the mixture comes to a steady simmer and continue to cook until you have a thick sauce.

At this point, it's time to add a bit of flavour, so add the wholegrain mustard, a pinch of nutmeg and three-quarters of the cheese, and season with sea salt and ground black pepper. Mix through until the cheese has melted. Pour the cheese sauce over the contents of the cooking pot and mix through until everything is combined.

Pour the contents of the pot into the baking dish, sprinkle with the remaining cheese and pop in the oven to cook for 25 minutes or until the top has turned golden and the sauce is bubbling up the sides. Remove from the oven and allow to cool slightly before serving in big, deep bowls.

RICH TOMATO ITALIAN
MEATBALLS WITH LINGUINE

If I was to name one recipe that is ideal food therapy, it's this. There is something extremely relaxing about rolling the meat into little balls and plopping them into a boiling, rich, tomato sauce. I rely solely on the heat of the sauce to cook and infuse the balls with flavour and I love to serve the dish on a big platter with serving spoons, so that people can dig in at the table.

 SERVES 4

500g (1lb 2oz) sausage meat

100g (3½oz) breadcrumbs

2 garlic cloves, peeled and minced

2 tsp Dijon mustard

2 tbsp tomato ketchup

1 tsp dried oregano

300g (11oz) good-quality linguine

Sea salt and ground black pepper

For the tomato sauce

1 tbsp olive oil

1 onion, peeled and finely chopped

1 garlic clove, peeled and finely chopped

2 x 400g (14oz) tins of chopped tomatoes

1 tsp Tabasco sauce

1 tsp dried oregano

½ glass red wine (about 150ml/5fl oz)

Place the sausage meat, breadcrumbs, garlic, mustard, ketchup and oregano in a large bowl with a good pinch of salt and pepper. Thoroughly mix everything together with a fork.

Wear plastic gloves or dip your hands in a bowl of cold water, then take about a teaspoonful of the mixture and roll with your hands into a small ball. (It's better to make the balls smaller as they will cook quicker and are a lot easier to eat.) Work your way through the mixture, setting the balls on a large baking tray. Place in the fridge to firm up.

To make the tomato sauce, heat a large saucepan over a medium–high heat, add the olive oil and fry the onion for 3 minutes, then add the garlic and fry for 1 minute. Add the tinned tomatoes, Tabasco, oregano and red wine and bring to the boil. Reduce the heat and allow to simmer for about 15 minutes or until the sauce has reduced, skimming off any oil as necessary. Season to taste with sea salt and ground black pepper.

Add the firmed-up meatballs to the saucepan, making sure they are covered by the sauce – this keeps the meat lovely and tender. Bring the sauce back to the boil and simmer for another 15 minutes.

Serve with the linguine, cooked according to the packet instructions, and there'll be clean plates all around!

CREAMY PORK KIDNEY
TAGLIATELLE

For most people, using offcuts like pork kidney might sound a little daunting, but I really want to encourage you to give this recipe a try. It makes a creamy and rich sauce for pasta. Your butcher will happily prepare the kidneys for you if you ask nicely.

 SERVES 4

5 pork kidneys

Juice of ½ lemon (or about 250ml/9fl oz buttermilk)

1 tbsp rapeseed oil

Generous knob of butter

1 onion, peeled and finely diced

2 garlic cloves, peeled and finely minced

200ml (7fl oz) beef stock

200ml (7fl oz) white wine

300g (11oz) tagliatelle

1 heaped tbsp wholegrain mustard

1 tarragon sprig, leaves finely chopped

50ml (2fl oz) single cream

Sea salt and ground black pepper

Crusty bread, to serve

Cut off the outer membrane from the pork kidneys, then slice them in half lengthways and use sharp kitchen scissors to snip away the white fat from the centre. Slice the kidneys into bite-sized pieces.

Submerge the pieces in a bowl of cold water with the lemon juice and allow to sit for about an hour. Alternatively, leave them to soak covered in buttermilk. This process will reduce the intense bitter flavour of the kidneys. Drain the kidney pieces, pat dry with kitchen paper and set aside.

Heat the oil and half the butter in a large frying pan until beginning to foam, then add the kidney pieces and brown them on all sides. Remove and set aside on a plate.

Melt the remaining butter in the frying pan until it begins to foam. Add the onion and fry for 3–5 minutes until soft, then add the garlic and fry for a further minute. Pour in the beef stock and white wine and bring to a steady simmer. Return the kidney pieces to the pan, cover and simmer gently for 40 minutes.

Ten minutes before the sauce is ready, bring a large cooking pot of water to the boil over a high heat and cook the tagliatelle until it's al dente.

Reduce the heat on the frying pan and add the mustard, tarragon and cream, stirring until incorporated. Season with sea salt and ground black pepper. Slowly simmer for a further 3 minutes or so.

Drain the pasta, and place back in the pot it was cooked in. Add the contents of the frying pan and mix through until combined. Serve in deep bowls with crusty bread to mop the plate clean.

LEFTOVER CHICKEN
CAESAR PASTA

This is one of my ultimate quick-fix suppers, a really tasty and substantial dish that makes the most of leftover chicken. It also makes a good lunchbox filler.

 SERVES 4–6

300g (11oz) macaroni

2 handfuls of sourdough bread, cut into cubes

2 tbsp olive oil, plus extra for the bread

4 tbsp mayonnaise

Juice of ½ lemon

1 large garlic clove, peeled

1 heaped tsp Dijon mustard

Good handful of freshly grated Parmesan cheese, plus extra to garnish

Shredded, cooked meat from ½ medium chicken (approx. 500g/1lb 2oz)

Sea salt and freshly ground pepper

Preheat the oven to 200°C (400°F), Gas Mark 6. Cook the macaroni according to the instructions on the packe, until al dente.

While the pasta is cooking, toss the cubes of bread in a little olive oil, put in a roasting tin and toast for 5–10 minutes in the oven until golden – keep an eye on them. Remove and set aside.

Whizz together the mayo, lemon juice, garlic, mustard, grated Parmesan, olive oil and a good pinch of sea salt and black pepper in a food processor until you have a smooth dressing. Toss the cooked chicken in any leftover juices that it was cooked in.

When the pasta is cooked, drain and tumble it back into the pot it was cooked in. Add the dressing, chicken and croûtons and stir until everything is combined. Serve straight away with a little extra sprinkle of Parmesan.

CHILLI TUNA
SPAGHETTI

Tuna is a fantastic, healthy, storecupboard ingredient which is perfect for quick dishes just like this. I really love the tuna that comes in jars or tins, stored in olive oil. Aim to buy sustainable line-caught tuna.

 SERVES 4

250g (9oz) wholemeal penne

2 tbsp olive oil

2 garlic cloves, peeled and finely minced

½ tsp chilli flakes

Good handful of flat-leaf parsley, roughly chopped

1 x 230g (8oz) jar of tuna fillets in olive oil

Sea salt and ground black pepper

Cook the pasta according to the instructions on the packet, until al dente.

In a large frying pan, heat the oil over a medium heat and add the garlic and chilli flakes. Fry gently until golden.

Add the cooked pasta and the parsley to the pan and toss until the pasta is nicely coated. Drain the tuna, saving just a little of the oil, and break the fish into rough chunks. Add to the pasta and stir through. Season with a good pinch of sea salt and black pepper and serve straight away.

SPICY TOMATO
& CHORIZO BAKED GNOCCHI

Gnocchi really is the epitome of comfort food – soft and tender little pillows of potato pasta, which really don't need much more than to be tossed in garlic butter and seasoned with sea salt and black pepper. Which is why I do feel I may be gilding the lily slightly with this baked version, but it really is delicious and makes a perfect comfort-food supper.

☛ SERVES 4

500g (1lb 2oz) fresh gnocchi

100g (3½oz) spicy chorizo sausage, finely chopped

1 tbsp olive oil (optional)

2 garlic cloves, peeled and finely chopped

1 onion, peeled and finely chopped

2 x 400g (14oz) tins of chopped tomatoes

½ tsp chilli flakes

1 tsp white sugar

2 x 125g (4½oz) mozzarella balls, sliced

Handful of basil leaves, torn

Sea salt and ground black pepper

Cook the gnocchi in a large pot of boiling water until they are tender and have risen to the surface, then drain and set aside.

In a large frying pan over a medium–high heat, fry the chorizo without any oil for 4 minutes until roaring-red and sizzling. It may release some of its own oil into the pan. Remove the chorizo with a slotted spoon and transfer to a plate lined with kitchen paper.

Add the tablespoon of olive oil to the frying pan if needed (as you may already have enough chorizo oil), set over a high heat and sauté the garlic and onion until soft. Add in the chopped tomatoes and chilli flakes and bring to the boil. Lower the heat and cook at a steady simmer for 15 minutes until the sauce has reduced. Add the sugar and season with sea salt and ground black pepper.

Preheat the oven to 200°C (400°F), Gas Mark 6. Tumble the gnocchi into the frying pan and stir them through the tomato sauce until each piece is nicely coated. Pour into a high-sided, 23cm (9in) square baking dish and top with the mozzarella slices and torn basil leaves.

Place in the oven for 25–30 minutes or until the top is nicely golden brown and bubbling. Serve straight away in deep bowls.

CREAMY SPINACH
GNOCCHI

One of my favourite quick-fix suppers, this is full of fresh flavours and has a nice hum of heat from the chilli flakes. Gnocchi is easy to make yourself, but you can now pick up packets of the fresh variety in most supermarkets. If you happen to have fresh peas growing in your garden, feel free to use them instead of frozen.

👉 SERVES 4 (V)

500g (1lb 2oz) fresh gnocchi

1 tbsp rapeseed oil

2 garlic cloves, peeled and finely chopped

Generous pinch of chilli flakes

150g (5oz) spinach

250ml (9fl oz) single cream

100g (3½oz) frozen peas

Grated zest of 1 lemon and juice of ½

Sea salt and ground black pepper

Bring a cooking pot of water to the boil, then add the gnocchi and cook for 2 minutes until they float to the top. Drain and set aside.

Place a large frying pan over a medium–high heat and add the oil. Fry the garlic and chilli flakes for 30 seconds or so before adding in the spinach. Allow the spinach to wilt down, tossing every now and then until the bulk has reduced.

Pour in the cream and add the peas. Bring to a steady simmer and cook for 5 minutes. Add the lemon zest and whisk in the lemon juice.

Add the cooked gnocchi, toss to combine and season with sea salt and ground black pepper. Serve straight away for a delicious and simple dinner.

MUSHY ROAST GARLIC SAUSAGE
& SPAGHETTI DINNER

The great thing about this one-tray meal is the mushy garlic and tomato sauce which coats the pasta. I know a whole bulb of garlic sounds like a lot, but roasting it mellows the flavour and so it is far less prominent than raw garlic would be. For a vegetarian version, drop the sausages and Parmesan cheese.

SERVES 4

200g (7oz) cherry tomatoes, sliced in half

1 red onion, peeled and quartered

8 good-quality thick sausages

1 garlic bulb, top sliced off

1 tbsp rapeseed oil

1 tbsp balsamic vinegar

1 tsp dried oregano

250g (9oz) wholegrain spaghetti

Sea salt and ground black pepper

Generous grating of Parmesan cheese, to serve

Preheat the oven to 200°C (400°F), Gas Mark 6. Arrange the tomatoes, onion and sausages in a large roasting tin. Try not to overcrowd the tin – allow enough space for the pieces to cook and caramelise.

Slice the top off the garlic bulb to expose the cloves and add the bulb to the tin. Drizzle the ingredients with the oil and balsamic vinegar, sprinkle with the oregano, sea salt and ground black pepper and place in the oven to roast for 35 minutes.

Fifteen minutes before the tin is due to come out of the oven, bring a large cooking pot of water to the boil over a high heat and cook the spaghetti until it's al dente.

When the cooking time is up, remove the roasting tin from the oven and allow to cool slightly before squeezing out the cloves from the garlic bulb and using the back of a fork to roughly mush them together with the tomatoes and onion. Check the seasoning and add more salt and pepper if you wish. Remove the sausages, cut into slices on the diagonal and set aside.

Drain the pasta and add to the tin, tossing it in the roughly mushed garlic, tomatoes and onion. Pop the sausages back into the tin. Dish up at the table using kitchen tongs and finish with a sprinkle of grated Parmesan cheese.

SPICY TOMATO SARDINE PASTA

This is a slightly more fishy twist on a puttanesca pasta sauce, using tinned sardines. It's a cheap, cheerful and ultimately satisfying supper made from storecupboard ingredients.

 SERVES 4

1 tbsp olive oil

3 garlic cloves, peeled and finely chopped

1 red chilli, deseeded and finely chopped

1 x 400g (14oz) tin of chopped tomatoes

½ glass of white wine (about 150ml/5fl oz)

350g (12oz) tagliatelle

2 x 112g (4oz) tins of sardines in tomato sauce

2 tbsp capers, rinsed

50g (2oz) green olives, pitted and halved

Grated zest of 1 lemon (juice to serve)

Sea salt and ground black pepper

Prepare the sauce by heating the oil in a medium frying pan over a high heat. Fry the garlic and chilli for about 1 minute until you can smell them. Add the tomatoes and white wine and bring to a steady simmer for 10 minutes.

Bring a large cooking pot of water to a steady boil over a high heat and cook the tagliatelle until al dente. Add the sardines (including their tomato sauce) to the pan and use a wooden spatula to press them down so that they break into small pieces.

Stir through the capers, olives and lemon zest and cook for a further 3 minutes. Season with sea salt and ground black pepper to taste.

When the pasta is cooked, drain and return it to the pot. Scrape the contents of the frying pan into the pot and gently mix through to combine. Serve straight away with a good squeeze of lemon juice to finish.

CREAMY BACON & MUSHROOM SPAGHETTI

This sauce can be made in the time it takes to boil the pasta — a proper 15-minute meal!

 SERVES 4

350g (12oz) spaghetti

Good knob of butter

150g (5oz) smoked streaky bacon, chopped into pieces

200g (7oz) button mushrooms

4 tbsp crème fraîche

Good handful of flat-leaf parsley, roughly chopped

Sea salt and ground black pepper

Bring a large cooking pot of water to the boil over a high heat and cook the spaghetti until al dente.

While the pasta is cooking, heat a medium non-stick frying pan over a medium–high heat and add the butter. Fry the bacon until just crisp. Add in the mushrooms and fry until tender. Mix through the crème fraîche until completely combined.

Quickly drain the pasta and place back in the pot, so that a tiny bit of cooking water still remains. Scrape in the contents of the frying pan and mix them through the spaghetti completely.

Season with sea salt and ground black pepper and stir through half the parsley. Serve with the rest of the parsley on top.

EVERYDAY EASY

SUPPERS

BAKING

PASTA

SIMPLE SIDES

CHEAP &

HEALTHY

SLOW-COOKED MEALS

SOUPS & STEWS

DESSERTS

№5

In most cases, side dishes tend to be a bit of an afterthought, just a little extra touch to sit beside the hero dish in a meal. This does not have to be the case, though, and most of the recipes in this chapter are good enough to stand alone as well as going really well with meat, chicken or fish.

A lot of the recipes here can essentially bring a dish together. For example, big, juicy slices of Porchetta, with its crispy crackling, are definitely best placed on top of some creamy, wholegrain mustard root-veg mash. The same goes for my Moroccan spiced lamb: the moist slices just wouldn't be the same without some lemon and chickpea couscous. For recipes in the book where I have not specified a side dish in the serving suggestions, many of the recipes from this section may be ideal. If you are entertaining, try to choose side dishes that can be made ahead, such as mash, oven bakes or a simple salad. You then have one less thing to think about, but when it comes to serving, your side dish will bring everything together. Most of the side dishes here are adaptable with different flavours, so do try to experiment.

Side dishes are also a great way to get greens into your diet – these recipes include just some of my favourite ways to enjoy veg. I like to serve a salad with most of the meals I cook, but I specifically haven't included salad recipes here because it is as simple as serving a few washed leaves with a quick dressing. Just combine 3 tablespoons of extra-virgin olive oil, 1 tablespoon of balsamic vinegar, a teaspoon of wholegrain mustard and a teaspoon of honey, shake it up in a jar and serve tossed through the salad leaves. Bar a few extra additions, like finely sliced red onion, feta cheese or a few cherry tomatoes, I don't think you need much else.

BOXTY COLCANNON
PANCAKES

Boxty potato pancakes are a traditional Irish recipe and they come with a great little rhyme that we were taught when growing up: 'Boxty on the griddle, boxty on the pan, the wee one in the middle is for Mary Ann.' The traditional recipe varies from region to region, but they all use grated raw potato. This is the version that my family makes and they are great with a full Irish breakfast, or I also serve them with pan-fried mackerel and a light salad.

 MAKES 8 PANCAKES (V)

250g (9oz) colcannon (see page 152) or mashed potato

250g (9oz) peeled, grated, raw rooster potatoes

100g (3½oz) plain flour

Up to 125ml (4½fl oz) milk

Knob of butter

Drop of rapeseed oil

Sea salt and ground black pepper

Put the colcannon, grated potatoes and flour in a bowl and mix until evenly combined. Add the milk, little by little, until you have a wet dropping consistency. Season to taste with sea salt and ground black pepper.

Heat a non-stick frying pan over a medium–high heat with a little butter and oil. When the butter begins to foam, spoon heaped tablespoon measurements of the mixture into the frying pan and fry for 3–4 minutes on each side until golden brown.

Remove from the pan and place on a plate lined with kitchen paper. Repeat with the remaining mixture. Serve the potato pancakes with fish, eggs, salad, etc.

AVOCADO & GARDEN
PEA MINT SALAD

This has to be one of my favourite summer salads. Invented solely to use up all the peas in my garden, it's a little superstar dish. You can of course use frozen peas here.

 **SERVES 4 (V)**

4 generous handfuls of shelled (or frozen) peas

Juice of ½ lemon

3 tbsp extra-virgin olive oil

2 avocados, halved, stoned and chopped into chunks

Small handful of mint leaves, finely sliced

Sea salt and ground black pepper

Put the peas into a pot of boiling water and cook for 2–3 minutes. Drain and plunge into ice-cold water.

In the bottom of a salad bowl, whisk together the lemon juice and olive oil, then add the avocado chunks, peas and mint. Gently toss the ingredients together until everything is evenly coated. Add a generous seasoning of sea salt and ground black pepper.

SWEDISH POTATO
JANSSON

Not unlike the French Potatoes Dauphinoise, this Swedish take features anchovies and matchstick potatoes. It's a regular at the Swedish Christmas table, but if you don't fancy the anchovies you can add some finely chopped garlic instead.

 SERVES 8

5 medium waxy potatoes, peeled and chopped into matchsticks (approx. 700g/1½lb)

14-16 Swedish anchovy fillets, brine reserved

2 large onions, peeled and sliced into half-moons

200ml (7fl oz) single cream

35g (1oz) butter

Small handful of fine breadcrumbs

Sea salt and ground black pepper

Preheat the oven to 220°C (425°F), Gas Mark 7. Put half the matchstick potatoes into a large, rectangular Pyrex or ovenproof dish. Evenly distribute the anchovy fillets and onions over the potatoes and top with the remaining potatoes.

Mix the cream with the anchovy brine; pour half of this over the layered potatoes, then dot the top with small knobs of the butter. Season with sea salt and ground black pepper. Place in the oven to cook for 20 minutes.

Remove from the oven, pour over the remaining cream and brine and scatter with the breadcrumbs. Place back in the oven and cook for a further 25–30 minutes or until the top is golden brown.

QUICK & EASY GREENS

It's important to get those greens into each meal, so here are a few ideas that are really simple and easy to prepare. All these recipes go well with dishes throughout the book, so try to stick them in wherever you can.

 **EACH SERVES 4–6**

Asian Greens (V)
Heat a large wok over a high heat and add a good lug of sunflower oil. Peel and finely mince a thumb-sized piece of fresh ginger, and add to the wok along with two finely minced garlic cloves. Fry for 30 seconds before adding three roughly shredded pak choi and half a head of roughly shredded Chinese cabbage. Stir-fry until the greens are tender, then drizzle with 1 tablespoon of light soy sauce and 1 teaspoon of sesame oil. Serve straight away.

Simple Spinach and Garlic (V)
Heat a large frying pan over a medium–high heat and add 1 tablespoon of olive oil. Fry two finely sliced garlic cloves for 30 seconds, then add 300g (11oz) spinach leaves and toss through until just wilted. Season with sea salt and ground black pepper and serve.

Broccoli (V)
Bring a medium pot of water to a boil over a high heat. Break a head of broccoli into florets, add to the pan and cook for 3–4 minutes or until tender when pierced with a fork. Drain completely, place in a bowl with a good knob of butter and season with sea salt and ground black pepper. Toss until the butter has melted completely. Serve straight away. I sometimes serve this with a quick, vegetarian Caesar dressing (see page 116).

Sugar Snap Peas (V)
Place a large frying pan over a medium–high heat and add a generous knob of butter and the grated zest of a lemon. When the butter is foaming, add 450g (1lb) sugar snap peas and stir-fry for 6–8 minutes. Season with sea salt and ground black pepper and serve straight away.

SIMPLE
ROOT VEG MASH

This is a healthy mash which goes well with any meat.

 **SERVES 4–6 (V)**

950g (2lb 2oz) sweet
potatoes, turnips and
parsnips, peeled and
chopped into 2.5cm
(1in) pieces

50g (2oz) butter

1 tsp honey

1 tbsp wholegrain mustard

Sea salt and ground
black pepper

Place the root vegetables into a cooking pot and fill it up with cold water. Place over a high heat and bring to the boil. Cook for 15–20 minutes or until the vegetable pieces are tender when pierced with a fork.

Drain the veg completely in a colander, then return it to the pot. Add the butter, honey and wholegrain mustard, and mash with a potato masher until completely smooth. Season with sea salt and ground black pepper and serve.

QUICK BEAN &
TOMATO STEW

I love substantial sides that can be easily prepared from storecupboard ingredients that I'm bound to have in the house. This quick bean and tomato stew is great with meat, poultry and fish – a total all-rounder!

 **SERVES 4** (V)
(if vegetable stock is used)

3 tbsp olive oil

2 onions, peeled and finely chopped

2 large carrots, peeled and finely chopped

2 celery stalks, trimmed and finely chopped

2 garlic cloves, peeled and finely chopped

1 bay leaf

2 thyme sprigs

1 litre (1¾ pints) chicken (or vegetable) stock

½ glass of white wine (about 150ml/5fl oz)

1 x 400g (14oz) tin of chopped tomatoes

2 x 400g (14oz) tins of cannellini beans, drained and rinsed

Handful of freshly chopped flat-leaf parsley (optional)

Heat the oil in a large, heavy cooking pot over a medium heat and fry the onions, carrots, celery, garlic, bay leaf and thyme for about 8 minutes, stirring occasionally, until all the vegetables are soft and tender.

Pour in the stock, wine and tomatoes and simmer for about 20 minutes or until the stew has reduced a little. Stir every few minutes and spoon off any froth that bubbles to the top.

Five minutes before serving, add the beans and stir through. Stir through some parsley, if you like, just before serving.

CHEESY POLENTA

Traditionally, polenta is not really a side dish, but it goes very nicely with slices of slow-roasted meat. Of course, these days you can buy quick-cook polenta, which you make according to the packet instructions and is an easier option, but it's a really nice and a slightly different taste when you make it from scratch using cornmeal. You can buy cornmeal in most supermarkets, otherwise health-food shops usually stock it.

 **SERVES 4 (V)**
(if vegetarian cheese is used)

200g (7oz) polenta (cornmeal)

35g (1oz) butter

75g (2½oz) Parmesan cheese, finely grated

Sea salt and ground black pepper

Bring 1 litre (1¾ pints) of water to the boil in a large pan. Pour in the polenta in a slow, steady stream and, using a wooden spoon, stir continuously until the contents of the pan come to a steady boil.

Reduce the heat to low and cook for 30–35 minutes until the liquid has been absorbed, the polenta has become thick and the grains are soft. Make sure to stir frequently so that the mixture doesn't catch on the bottom of the pan. Add a little extra water if the grains aren't tender after 35 minutes.

Finally, stir in the butter and grated Parmesan and season with sea salt and ground black pepper. Serve while still hot.

BOULANGÈRE POTATOES

In French villages, after the local bakery had finished baking the bread for the day, locals would hand over their casseroles of potatoes to the baker to use the remaining heat in the ovens to cook the vegetables slowly overnight. Hence the name Boulangère, the French word for 'baker'. Similar to its creamy cousin Potatoes Dauphinoise, this dish uses layers of potatoes but is far more economical, using stock to cook it instead of cream.

 **SERVES 4–6 (V)**
(if vegetable stock is used)

Generous knob of butter

2 onions, peeled and finely sliced

2 garlic cloves, peeled and finely minced

1kg (2lb 3oz) waxy potatoes, peeled and finely sliced

425ml (15fl oz) chicken or vegetable stock

2 thyme sprigs, leaves stripped

Sea salt and ground black pepper

Place a medium, non-stick frying pan over a medium-high heat, add a little of the butter and gently fry the onions and garlic for about 8 minutes until soft and lightly coloured.

Preheat the oven to 180°C (350°F), Gas Mark 4. Use butter to grease a 1.5 litre (2½ pint) rectangular or oval baking dish and layer the potatoes across the base. Place a layer of the onion and garlic on top and repeat the process until you finish with a layer of potatoes.

Mix together the stock and thyme leaves; pour this over the potatoes and onion. Season the top with sea salt and ground black pepper.

Place in the oven and cook for 55–60 minutes or until the potatoes are tender when pierced with a fork and golden brown on top.

ROAST CABBAGE

Don't knock this recipe until you've tried it. If you have horrible memories of overcooked cabbage for school dinners, this recipe will rock your world. Roasting the cabbage brings out its true beauty, with a sweet and smoky flavour.

 **SERVES 4 (V)**

1 sweetheart cabbage, core removed and the rest cut into quarters

35g (1oz) butter

2 tbsp olive oil

Sea salt and ground black pepper

Preheat the oven to 220°C (425°F), Gas Mark 7. Place the cabbage quarters in a roasting tin with their cut sides up. Spread the butter onto the cut sides and drizzle with olive oil. Season with sea salt and ground black pepper.

Roast in the oven for 25 minutes or until tender when pierced with a fork. If the edges begin to char too much, simply cover the dish with foil. Serve straight away as a tasty veggie side.

NUTTY VEGGIE
SATAY NOODLES

The rest of this dish is really secondary to the amazing peanut sauce, which is incredibly versatile and can be used with chicken and meat. You can add grated carrots, finely sliced cucumber and peppers if you want to up the veggies here.

👉 SERVES 4 (V)

400g (14oz) rice vermicelli noodles

1 red pepper, finely sliced

1 yellow pepper, finely sliced

5 spring onions, finely sliced diagonally

Handful of salted peanuts, roughly chopped

For the peanut sauce

1 tbsp sunflower oil

1 garlic clove, peeled and finely minced

1 small thumb-sized piece of fresh ginger, peeled and finely minced

1 small red chilli, deseeded and finely chopped

200ml (7fl oz) coconut milk

Juice of 1 lime

3 tbsp crunchy peanut butter

½ tbsp dark soy sauce

Cook the noodles according to the instructions on the packet, then rinse under cold water, drain and set aside.

To make the peanut sauce, heat the oil in a small pan, add the garlic, ginger and chilli and fry for 30–40 seconds, stirring continuously. Add the coconut milk, lime juice, peanut butter and soy sauce. Bring to the boil, stirring to melt the peanut butter, then reduce the heat and simmer for 2–3 minutes.

Put the cooked noodles in a large mixing bowl with the peppers and add most of the spring onions, saving a few to use as a garnish. Pour in the peanut sauce and toss all the ingredients together until combined. Serve with a sprinkle of chopped peanuts and the remaining sliced spring onion.

HERBY HASSELHOFF
POTATOES

This version of hasselback potatoes is possibly one of the sides most requested by my family and friends, so much so that it is now lovingly nicknamed Hasselhoff Potatoes. It is essentially a stripped-back version of a Swedish classic. You can play around with flavours here – try adding chilli for a kick of spice.

 **SERVES 4 (V)**

Approx. 20 baby potatoes

2 garlic cloves, peeled and finely minced

1 rosemary sprig, leaves finely chopped

1 thyme sprig, leaves finely chopped

2 tbsp melted butter

Generous pinch of coarse sea salt

Preheat the oven to 200°C (400°F), Gas Mark 6. Place each potato in the dip of a wooden spoon and repeatedly cut slices right across the potato, about 3mm (⅛in) apart; the dip in the spoon will prevent you slicing all the way through.

When you're finished, place all the potatoes in a roasting tray, sliced-side up. Mix the garlic and herbs with the melted butter and brush it onto each potato, then add a good sprinkling of coarse sea salt.

Roast for 45–50 minutes or until the slices in the potatoes fan out and turn golden brown. Serve straight away, whilst hot, or they can also be served at room temperature.

BAKED FENNEL

Apart from using it raw in salads, this is one of my favourite ways of enjoying fennel, which has a wonderful and unique aniseed flavour.

 **SERVES 4** (V)
(if vegetarian cheese is used)

Large knob of butter

Good glug of rapeseed oil

2 large fennel bulbs, sliced into quarters

Good grating of Parmesan cheese

Sea salt and ground black pepper

Preheat the oven to 200°C (400°F), Gas Mark 6. Add the butter and oil to a large frying pan over a medium-high heat. Fry the fennel until it has a nice golden colour on all sides.

Transfer the fennel to a baking dish. Season with sea salt and ground black pepper and cover with foil. Pop in the oven to cook for 25–30 minutes or until tender.

Remove the fennel from the oven and scatter over the Parmesan cheese. Pop it back in the oven until the top is golden. Serve it straight away.

COLCANNON
MASH

Every time I mention Colcannon to my granddad, he bursts into song:

Well, did you ever make colcannon, made with lovely pickled cream?
With the greens and scallions mingled like a picture in a dream.
Did you ever make a hole on top to hold the meltin' flake?
Or the creamy flavoured butter that our mothers used to make?

It's a traditionally Irish dish made around Halloween with mashed potatoes and is a wonderful side for lots of different dishes. You can make it with kale, which is traditional, or Savoy cabbage, which can be more readily available throughout the year.

 **SERVES 4** (V)

1kg (2lb 3oz) floury
potatoes, peeled and diced

250g (9oz) Savoy cabbage,
finely sliced

35g (1oz) butter

75ml (2½fl oz) milk
or single cream, plus
a little extra if required

Bunch of spring onions,
finely sliced

Sea salt and ground
black pepper

Put the potatoes in a cooking pot of cold water, cover, place over a high heat and bring to the boil. Reduce the heat and simmer for 20–25 minutes or until the potatoes are tender when pierced with a fork.

Add a little water to another pot, place a metal steamer inside and bring the water to the boil. Place the cabbage into the steamer and steam for 2–3 minutes until tender.

When the potatoes are cooked, remove from the heat and drain in a colander, then return them to the pot along with the butter and milk. (You may want to add a little bit more or less milk and butter – it's up to you.) Allow the butter and milk to warm through from the heat of the potatoes, then use a potato masher to mash them until smooth and creamy.

Add the spring onion, steamed cabbage and a good pinch of sea salt and black pepper, and stir all these through with a spoon until evenly combined.

LEMON CHICKPEA
COUSCOUS

This is a perfect summer side dish and is wonderfully versatile. I particularly like to serve a big bowl of it at barbecues.

 **SERVES 4 (V)**

250g (9oz) couscous

400ml (14fl oz) hot vegetable stock

1 x 400g (14oz) tin of chickpeas, drained and rinsed

Grated zest of 1 lemon

150g (5oz) feta cheese

For the dressing

3 tbsp extra-virgin olive oil

1 tbsp lemon juice

1 tsp Dijon mustard

1 garlic clove, peeled and finely chopped

Sea salt and ground black pepper

Whisk together the ingredients for the dressing and set aside.

Put the couscous in a bowl and pour over the hot stock. Cover the bowl with cling film and leave for 5 minutes or until all the water has been soaked up and the couscous is nice and plump.

Use a fork to fluff up the couscous when it's ready. Toss in the chickpeas, along with the dressing, lemon zest and feta cheese. Serve straight away or leave to sit for a little to allow the flavours to develop.

EVERYDAY EASY

SUPPERS

BAKING

PASTA

SIMPLE SIDES

CHEAP &

HEALTHY

SLOW COOKED MEALS
SOUPS & STEWS

DESSERTS

№6

It could be argued that a chapter on desserts might be out of place in a cookbook focusing on budget-conscious recipes, but any cook will know, despite budgets, that there is always room for something sweet. More often than not, homemade desserts are more affordable than shop-bought ones and the end result is ultimately superior. All the recipes here are made using accessible ingredients that are easy to get hold of. A couple of the desserts may be slightly pricier to make, but remember that any expense will be spread out between six, eight or even twelve people and therefore becomes worth the cost.

Simple desserts are often the most impressive, so you needn't worry about breaking the bank to serve up something delicious. Some of my favourite dessert recipes simply use up leftover fruit such as apples and bananas. In fact, you will find that unappealing and rapidly blackening banana in your fruit bowl is far more suited to a baking recipe than a fresh one will ever be.

I love desserts that can be made in advance, and when I make dinner for a crowd, the dessert is often the thing I start with, leaving me safe in the knowledge that something sweet is ready to serve when I need it. Recipes like my Steamed Banana Puds with Salted Caramel Sauce, Mini Molten Chocolate Puddings, Rhubarb Panna Cotta and Dark Chocolate Espresso Cups can all be prepared in advance and cooked or presented when you are ready for them.

ZESTY ORANGE
PUDDINGS

These are rather elegant little puddings that use mostly storecupboard baking ingredients. Steaming them makes the sponge wonderfully moist.

👉 MAKES 6

125g (4½oz) butter, plus extra for greasing

125g (4½oz) caster sugar

2 large free-range eggs

225g (8oz) self-raising flour

150ml (5fl oz) milk

1 tsp vanilla extract

Grated zest and juice of 2 oranges

1 thumb-sized piece of fresh ginger, peeled and finely grated

90ml (3fl oz) golden syrup

Preheat the oven to 180°C (350°F), Gas Mark 4. Grease six individual pudding moulds or ramekins. Place in a high-sided baking tin and set aside

In a standalone mixer (or in a large bowl, using an electric hand mixer), beat the butter and sugar until light and pale. Scrape down the sides of the bowl, then add the eggs one at a time, beating until combined.

Sift in the flour and whisk until combined. Pour in the milk and vanilla extract and whisk until they are completely incorporated. Stir through the zest of one orange and the ginger, then divide the mixture between the greased pudding moulds.

Pour boiling water about halfway up the sides of the ramekins, taking care not to splash yourself, and cover the baking tin loosely with tin foil, shiny side down. Carefully transfer to the middle shelf of the oven and cook for 35-40 minutes, until a skewer inserted into the centre of one of the puddings comes out clean.

For the sauce, place the golden syrup, orange juice and remaining zest in a small saucepan. Bring to the boil over a medium–high heat and cook for approximately 6–8 minutes until the sauce becomes thick and syrupy.

Remove the puddings when they are cooked and serve with a drizzle of the syrupy orange sauce.

JAM JUMBLE CRUMBLE TART

This tart is a real lifesaver; it uses solely kitchen staple ingredients and is very easy to assemble. It reminds me of the little tarts I used to make when I first started baking, but it is a bit more sophisticated and I love the addition of desiccated coconut, which goes well with the jam. You can use whatever jam you have in your cupboard – all flavours work perfectly.

 SERVES 6–8

100g (3½oz) desiccated coconut

100g (3½oz) caster sugar

150g (5oz) butter, cold

250g (9oz) plain flour

2 tbsp beaten egg

1 tsp vanilla extract (optional)

340g (12oz) raspberry jam

Whipped cream or vanilla ice cream, to serve

Preheat the oven to 200°C (400°F), Gas Mark 6. Place the coconut, sugar, butter and flour in a food processor and blitz until the mixture resembles breadcrumbs.

Remove roughly 180g (6½oz) of the mixture and set aside for the topping. Add the egg to the remaining pastry mixture along with the vanilla extract, if using, and blitz until the dough begins to clump together.

Press the dough into the base and sides of a 23cm (9in) tart tin, 2.5cm (1in) in depth and with a removable base, until you have a smooth surface. Place in the oven on the middle shelf to bake for 10–12 minutes.

Mix the jam with a spoon to loosen it. Remove the tart tin from the oven and spread the jam across the base. Use your fingertips to form little clumps of the reserved pastry mix and put these on top of the tart. Pop it back in the oven to cook for 15 minutes until the topping is golden brown.

Take the tart out of the oven and allow it to cool on a wire rack before removing from the tin and placing on a serving platter. Serve slices with freshly whipped cream or some good-quality vanilla ice cream.

SOFIE'S RHUBARB
PANNA COTTA

When my girlfriend Sofie was growing up, her grandparents had one of the most amazing vegetable gardens in Sweden, with wild strawberries and big, bushy apple trees. Huge rhubarb plants still spring up every year and the last time we visited I made this creamy panna cotta, which is a wonderful way to enjoy some of the summer's finest rhubarb.

 SERVES 6

1 litre (1¾ pints)
single cream

60g (2oz) caster sugar

2 vanilla pods, split
and seeds scraped
(or 1 tsp vanilla extract)

10g gelatin leaves
(individual leaves
vary in weight so check
packet for info)

For the rhubarb
900g (2lb) rhubarb

100g (3½oz) caster sugar

Grated zest and juice
of 1 orange (200ml/
7fl oz juice)

Place the cream, sugar, vanilla pods and seeds in a saucepan over a medium-high heat and bring to a gentle simmer. Stir until the sugar has dissolved, then remove from the heat. Meanwhile, place the gelatin sheets in a Pyrex or glass dish and cover with a little water. Leave to stand for 5 minutes until the gelatin has softened.

Remove the softened gelatin from the liquid and squeeze out any excess. Remove the vanilla pods from the warmed cream, then add the softened gelatin and stir through until dissolved. Divide the mixture amongst six pudding moulds, cover with cling film and place in the fridge to set for a few hours.

Cut the rhubarb into 6cm (2½in) pieces. Place the sugar, orange zest and juice in a cooking pot with 100ml (3½fl oz) water, place over a medium-high heat and bring to a steady simmer, stirring until the sugar is dissolved. Add the rhubarb to the pot and poach until it is soft when pierced with a fork. Remove with a slotted spoon and set aside on a plate.

Continue to cook the poaching liquid until it becomes syrupy. Remove from the heat and allow to cool slightly before adding the rhubarb back in.

To remove the panna cotta from the moulds, fill a bowl with warm water and dip them in. The heat will loosen the puddings slightly and allow them to be inverted onto serving plates. Serve each panna cotta with a few tablespoons of the rhubarb mix.

SALTED
CARAMEL SLICES

My granddad used to buy packets of these to take with us on rainy days spent on his boat. The bought ones were never nearly as nice as the ones we made ourselves with dense caramel, a rich shortbread base and a perfect chocolate top.

 **MAKES 16 SQUARES**

For the shortbread base
100g (3½oz) butter, plus extra for greasing
250g (9oz) self-raising flour
50g (2oz) caster sugar

For the topping
200g (7oz) caster sugar
½ tsp sea salt
4 tbsp golden syrup
200g (7oz) butter
1 x 400g (14oz) tin of condensed milk
200g (7oz) dark chocolate, roughly chopped

Preheat the oven to 180°C (350°F), Gas Mark 4. Grease a 33 x 23 x 5cm (13 x 9 x 2in) baking tin with butter.

In a bowl, use your fingertips to rub together the butter and flour for the shortbread base, then mix in the sugar. Press the mixture into the baking tin and bake in the oven for 20 minutes or until lightly golden. Leave the oven turned on.

While the base is cooking, prepare the salted caramel. Place all the topping ingredients, except the chocolate, in a saucepan over a low-medium heat and allow to melt, then bring to the boil and simmer for 10–15 minutes until you have achieved a nice toffee colour, stirring regularly to ensure the sauce doesn't catch on the bottom of the pan.

Pour the caramel over the shortbread base and place back in the oven to cook for 10 minutes. When done, remove the baking tin from the oven and allow to cool completely.

Melt the chocolate in a heatproof bowl set over a pan of shallow simmering water, then pour the melted chocolate over the cooled caramel and spread evenly with a palette knife. Once the chocolate has set, slice into 16 squares, or smaller ones if you want them to stretch further.

LAST-MINUTE DARK
CHOCOLATE ESPRESSO CUPS

I think every cook needs a dessert recipe like this, which can be made in a matter of minutes just before you start cooking the main meal. Try to use the best-quality chocolate you can afford – in a recipe like this, where it's the star attraction, it is very important.

 SERVES 6

200g (7oz) dark chocolate, chopped

300ml (10½fl oz) single cream

3 green cardamom pods, split and contents ground

2 tbsp cold espresso

Melt the chocolate slowly in a heatproof bowl sitting over a pan of gently simmering water. When melted, remove the bowl from the heat and pour 100ml (3½fl oz) of the hot water into a measuring jug.

Pour a little of this water at a time into the melted chocolate and stir through completely after each addition until you have added it all. It's important to do this slowly as adding all the water at once will result in the chocolate splitting.

Stir through 100ml (3½fl oz) of the cream, the ground cardamom and espresso until they are evenly incorporated. Divide the mixture amongst six small serving glasses or cups and place in the fridge to set for 30 minutes.

Meanwhile, whip the remaining cream. When you're ready to serve, offer the cream on the table or add tablespoons of the whipped cream to the top of the chocolate pots.

BIG DO'S TINNED PEACH & BLACKBERRY COBBLER

My granddad Do used to keep me and my cousins entertained all summer long on his boat with fishing, crab races and stories about pirates, deep-sea treasure and the biggest fish he ever caught! He liked his food, but never cooked – on our summer adventures with him we were always under strict orders to bring sandwiches! One day, I caught him sitting below deck slurping peaches in syrup from the tin, one of his favourite after-lunch treats, so this recipe is dedicated to him!

SERVES 4–6

2 x 420g (15oz) tins of peaches, peaches cut into quarters

300g (11oz) blackberries

4 tbsp caster sugar

4 tbsp soft light brown sugar, plus extra for sprinkling

1 tbsp cornflour

½ tsp ground cloves

Juice of ½ orange

Whipped cream or good-quality vanilla ice cream, to serve

For the pastry

100g (3½oz) cold butter, cut into cubes

250g (9oz) self-raising flour

4 tbsp caster sugar

150ml (5fl oz) milk, plus extra for brushing

1 tsp vanilla extract

Grated zest of 1 orange

Preheat the oven to 220°C (425°F), Gas Mark 7. Place the peaches, blackberries, both sugars, cornflour, ground cloves and orange juice in a large Pyrex or ovenproof baking dish and toss together until combined.

Make the pastry in a large bowl, using your fingertips to rub the butter into the flour and sugar until the mixture resembles rough breadcrumbs. Add the milk, vanilla extract and orange zest and stir through with a wooden spoon until you have a rough dough.

Using your hands, form rough, palm-sized balls of dough and arrange them on top of the peaches and blackberries. Brush the cobbler balls with milk and sprinkle with light brown sugar.

Place in the oven on the middle shelf. After 5 minutes, turn the heat down to 180°C (350°F), Gas Mark 4 and cook for 50–60 minutes until golden brown on top and the fruit juices seep up the sides. If you find that the topping starts to colour too much before the end of the cooking time, simply cover the dish with foil.

Remove from the oven and allow to cool slightly. Serve warm with freshly whipped cream or some good-quality vanilla ice cream.

STICKY TOFFEE BANANA PUDS WITH
SALTED CARAMEL SAUCE

Now, I know I shouldn't do this, but if I had to choose my absolute favourite dessert in this book, it would be this. It's essentially a sticky toffee pudding with banana and is incredibly rich, though I could probably eat about four of them in one sitting. Adding the sea salt to the caramel sauce might sound strange but it actually balances the sweetness and heightens the flavour. You can make the puds and sauce up to a week in advance; both will keep really well. Make sure to serve them hot.

SERVES 10

160g (5½oz) butter,
plus extra for greasing

175g (6oz) stoned dates,
chopped

190g (6½oz) soft light
brown sugar

2 large free-range eggs

1 tsp bicarbonate of soda

200g (7oz) self-raising flour

2 bananas, mashed

1 tsp vanilla extract

**For the salted
caramel sauce**

100g (3½oz) butter

150g (5oz) soft dark
brown sugar

3 tbsp golden syrup

150ml (5fl oz) double cream

1 tsp vanilla extract

Generous pinch of sea salt

Preheat the oven to 180°C (350°F), Gas Mark 4. Grease 10 small pudding moulds and divide them between two baking sheets.

Put the dates and 300ml (10½fl oz) water in a saucepan and place over a medium–high heat. Bring the mixture to the boil and then simmer for approximately 20 minutes or until the liquid has reduced by half and the dates have completely softened.

Cream the butter and sugar in a large bowl with an electric hand mixer until light and pale. Add one egg at a time, mixing after each addition, until they are incorporated. (If you add the eggs all at once, the mixture can split.)

Blitz the dates with a hand blender while still hot, until smooth, then stir through the bicarbonate of soda. Fold the date mixture, flour, bananas and vanilla extract into the pudding mixture until you have a smooth batter. Divide the mixture between the 10 moulds and bake in the oven for 20–25 minutes.

Meanwhile, make the salted caramel sauce. Place the butter, sugar and golden syrup in a saucepan and bring to a gentle boil until the sugar is dissolved. Add the cream, vanilla extract and salt and whisk together. Bring to a steady simmer for 3 minutes until the sauce is sticky and thick.

Insert a metal skewer into the centre of one of the puddings; if it comes out clean, the puddings are ready. Remove from the oven and allow to cool slightly before inverting them onto serving plates. Serve covered in the hot salted caramel sauce.

CROWD-PLEASING FAMILY TRIFLE

I love the drama and tension of a trifle – the oohs and the aahs when you present the colossal dessert to the table, followed by the slurping as it's eaten. Save this one for very special occasions.

 **SERVES 10–12**

270g (9½oz) strawberry jelly

500g (1lb 2oz) store-bought sponge cake

500ml (18fl oz) double cream

60g (2oz) flaked almonds

100ml (3½fl oz) sherry

For the custard

560ml (19½fl oz) milk

1 vanilla pod, split and seeds scraped (or 1 tsp vanilla extract)

60g (2oz) caster sugar

4 egg yolks

2 tbsp cornflour

Make the jelly according to the instructions on the packet and pour into a 20cm (8in) trifle dish (capacity 3.25 litres/5½ pints). Cover with cling film and place in the fridge to set completely while you prepare the rest of the layers.

Make the custard by placing the milk and vanilla pod and seeds in a small pan over a medium–high heat and bringing to a vigorous simmer. While the milk is heating, whisk together the sugar, egg yolks and cornflour in a large bowl.

When the milk is hot, slowly pour it into the egg mixture, whisking continuously until combined. Transfer the mixture back into the pan and place over a low heat, stirring every now and then for 6 minutes until the custard is thickened and coats the back of a wooden spoon.

Remove the custard from the heat and place a sheet of cling film directly on top of it to prevent a skin from forming. Set aside and allow to cool completely.

Trim off the top, bottom and edges of the sponge cake with a bread knife to match up with the trifle dish. You want it to fit quite snugly so that the toppings don't drip down the sides. Whip the cream in a large bowl until it just forms peaks; place in the fridge until you are ready to assemble.

Toast the almonds in a frying pan over a medium–high heat for about 3 minutes. Make sure not to burn them. Remove to a plate and allow to cool completely.

Once the jelly has set, carefully layer the trimmed sponge cake on top of the jelly. You can cut it into quarters for easier assembly if you wish. Douse with the sherry, top with custard and then with whipped cream. You can place the trifle back in the fridge at this stage or serve straight away with a sprinkle of toasted almonds.

RICE-KRISPIE CARAMEL SWIRL
ICE-CREAM CAKE

This very cool ice-cream cake comes with a warning: once you make it, you're going to want it again and again and again! It's lots of fun to make and a perfect one for kids to have a go at. As it serves quite a few people, it's ideal for birthday parties and family gatherings. When you melt the chocolate, be careful to do so over a low heat so that it doesn't go grainy. The caramel can also be made using a tin of condensed milk, boiled for 2 hours in water at a steady simmer – make sure the water is continuously at least 2.5cm (1in) above the top of the unopened tin. Allow to cool before using.

☛ SERVES 8–10

250g (9oz) good-quality milk chocolate, roughly chopped

75g (2½oz) Rice Krispies

2 x 500ml (18fl oz) tubs of good-quality vanilla ice cream

200g (7oz) tinned caramel (dulce de leche)

Place a cooking pot with about 2cm (¾in) of water over a medium heat, place the chocolate into a heatproof bowl and sit the bowl over the pot without it touching the water. Allow the chocolate to melt slowly, making sure none of the steam escapes up the sides and into the chocolate, as this will cause it to go grainy. You may want to reduce the heat to low once the water begins to simmer.

Place the Rice Krispies in a bowl, and when the chocolate is melted, pour it in and mix until combined. Press the mixture into the base and sides of a 23cm (9in) round cake tin with a removable base. Place in the freezer to firm up for about 10 minutes.

Take the ice cream out of the freezer and allow it to soften slightly at room temperature so that it's easy to spread. Scoop the ice cream into a bowl and gently fold through the caramel until you have nice swirls. Try not to overmix as you want to see the swirls distinctly when you cut through the cake.

Spread the ice cream on the Rice-Krispie base and place in the freezer, covered in foil, for about 2 hours until set. Remove from the freezer about 8 minutes before you plan to serve.

MINI MOLTEN
CHOCOLATE PUDDINGS

Chocolate and chilli might sound like an odd combination, but sweet and spicy do work together. I first tried the combination in hot chocolate. It's a subtle heat that you can taste, but instead of dominating the dessert it's an interesting extra note that adds to the flavour of the chocolate. However, do feel free to leave the chilli out if you prefer. These puds have an oozing liquid chocolate interior and can be made in advance and placed in the fridge until you are ready to bake them allowing approximately an extra five minutes cooking time.

 SERVES 6

175g (6oz) butter, plus extra for greasing

100g (3½oz) dark chocolate, chopped

3 large free-range eggs

125g (4½oz) caster sugar

30g (1oz) plain flour

½ tsp chilli powder (optional)

Whipped cream, to serve

Preheat the oven to 180°C (350°F), Gas Mark 4. Grease six mini pudding moulds.

Melt the butter in a saucepan. Remove from the heat and gently stir through the chopped chocolate until melted.

In a medium-sized mixing bowl, whisk together the eggs and sugar until they become pale and thick. Pour in the chocolate mixture, then sift in the flour and chilli powder, if using. Using a spatula, fold the mixture together until it is evenly combined.

Place the greased pudding moulds on a baking sheet and divide the chocolate batter amongst them. Place in the oven on the middle shelf to cook for 12 minutes. When cooked, remove from the oven and leave to rest for at least 1 minute. Then run a mini spatula around the inside edges to loosen the puddings, invert onto plates and serve immediately with freshly whipped cream.

MOM'S BREAD & BUTTER
ORCHARD PUD

When I was growing up, I couldn't understand why you would possibly want to eat bread and butter for dessert. After some explaining and a story about how my granny would make the best desserts from very little, my mom decided the easiest thing was for me to taste it. This was the recipe she made, which I've been cooking ever since. The apple slices are a recent addition of mine and make it the perfect autumnal pud. This dessert is great for using up any leftover bread.

SERVES 6

60g (2oz) butter, plus extra for greasing

8 thick slices of stale white bread, crusts removed

80g (3oz) marmalade

1 large cooking apple, peeled and cored, sliced very thinly

125g (4½oz) caster sugar

1 tsp ground cinnamon

Pinch of freshly grated nutmeg

850ml (1½ pints) milk

3 large free-range eggs

1 tsp vanilla extract

Pouring cream, to serve

Grease a 20 x 12cm (8 x 5in) ovenproof baking dish with a little butter. Butter each slice of bread on one side and spread with a little marmalade. Make into sandwiches and cut into quarters on the diagonal.

Arrange the sandwich quarters upright in the dish, with their longest side down and the opposite corner pointing upwards. Tuck the apple slices in between them. Mix 75g (2½oz) of the sugar with the cinnamon and nutmeg, and sprinkle this mixture over the apple and bread as you arrange the slices.

In a large jug, whisk together the milk, eggs and vanilla extract until combined. Pour this mixture over the bread and apple slices and press the slices gently with your fingertips so that the bread soaks up the liquid.

Sprinkle the top with the remaining sugar, cover with cling film and set aside for 25 minutes or so until the bread has soaked up a lot of the liquid.

Preheat the oven to 160°C (325°F), Gas Mark 3. Bake the pudding in the oven for approximately 50–55 minutes until the top has puffed up and turned a nice golden colour. Allow to cool slightly before serving with a little pouring cream.

EVERYDAY EASY SUPPERS

SIMPLE SIDES

CHEAP & HEALTHY

SLOW-COOKED MEALS

SOUPS & STEWS

BAKING

☞ BAKING

PASTA

DESSERTS

№7

I have a particular fondness for baking and it never fails to keep me interested. I'm always on the lookout on my travels for fresh and exciting ideas, but it's often the traditional baking recipes – the ones I grew up with – that I come back to. Flapjacks, scones, Irish Barmbrack and apple cake are all recipes that instantly remind me of being in the kitchen, cooking with my mom.

I have to confess to having a sweet tooth, and when I was growing up, I used to love it when my auntie Ann came back from America with baking cookbooks filled to the brim with completely over-the-top recipes for buttercream-frosted cakes, sweet blueberry muffins and chewy chocolate chip cookies. I would spend hours upon hours trawling through them and choosing my favourites to try out.

Baking definitely wasn't an everyday event in our house when I was growing up, which is why it has always been special for me. It marked an occasion – a visit from an old friend, grandparents coming for lunch, something to take with us on a long car ride, or even just an urge to produce something sweet on a cold winter's day when there was nothing else in the house.

The recipes in this chapter will all feed a crowd and are perfect for any of those big events, such as birthdays and family gatherings, which everyone is faced with throughout the year.

SWEDISH KLADDKAKA (GOOEY CHOCOLATE CAKE)

If you're looking for a gooey chocolate fix, you've come to the right place. This cake is perfect for a quick dessert and uses basic ingredients that you probably already have in your storecupboard.

 SERVES 8

100g (3½oz) butter, plus extra for greasing

70g (2½oz) plain flour, plus extra for dusting

200g (7oz) caster sugar

2 large free-range eggs

3 tbsp cocoa powder

1 tsp vanilla extract

Icing sugar, to dust

Whipped cream, to serve

Preheat the oven to 180°C (350°F), Gas Mark 4. Grease a 24cm (9½in) cake tin with a removable base, dust with flour and set aside.

Melt the butter in a saucepan. Remove from the heat, add the sugar and eggs and mix well. Add the flour, cocoa and vanilla and mix until combined.

Pour into the prepared cake tin and place in the oven for 20 minutes. The cake won't rise dramatically but you should be left with a set top and gooey middle.

Serve in slices, with a dusting of icing sugar over the top and a little whipped cream.

LEMON SLICES

The perfect accompaniment to a nice cup of tea, these lemon drizzle slices are light and zesty, and a good alternative for those who don't particularly love heavy cake. If you aren't too keen on baking, this all-in-one recipe makes things very simple and gives impressive results.

 MAKES 30

250g (9oz) self-raising flour
1 tsp baking powder
225g (8oz) caster sugar
4 large free-range eggs
225g (8oz) butter, at room temperature
3 tbsp milk
Grated zest of 3 lemons

For the lemon drizzle
200g (7oz) icing sugar
Grated zest and juice of 1 lemon

Preheat the oven to 160°C (325°F), Gas Mark 3. Line a 30 x 23cm (12 x 9in) rectangular baking tin with parchment paper.

Place all the dry ingredients in a large bowl and make a well in the middle with the back of a spoon. Add the eggs, butter, milk and lemon zest and beat with an electric hand mixer until well combined, for about 2 minutes.

Pour the mixture into the lined tin, place on the middle rack in the oven and cook for 35 minutes until risen and golden brown on top. Turn out onto a wire rack and allow to cool completely before icing.

Whisk together the ingredients for the drizzle and spread over the top of the cooled lemon cake. Allow to set for about 1 hour before slicing into 30 pieces.

'MOM WON'T GO TO THE SHOPS' SCONES

When we were growing up, on evenings when there was 'nothing in the house', a phrase that my brother and I used to complain to my mom on a regular basis, she would always make scones sprinkled with a little sugar. Warm from the oven, smothered in butter and jam, and eaten in the kitchen, they would always beat even the most amazing packet of sweets.

 MAKES 8

250g (9oz) self-raising flour, plus extra for dusting

1 tsp baking powder

60g (2oz) butter

60g (2oz) caster sugar, plus extra for sprinkling

3 tbsp milk, plus extra for brushing

1 egg

Preheat the oven to 220°C (425°F), Gas Mark 7. Dust a large baking sheet with flour.

Combine the flour and baking powder in a large mixing bowl and, using your fingertips, rub in the butter until the mixture resembles rough breadcrumbs. Add the sugar to the bowl and mix it through the crumbs.

In a measuring jug, whisk together the milk and egg until combined. Pour this into the crumb mixture and mix through with a table knife until a rough dough forms. Use your hands to push the dough together, making sure to include any mixture that's stuck on the sides of the bowl.

Dust a clean work surface with a little flour, turn the dough out of the bowl and press into a round shape. With a rolling pin, roll the dough out to a thickness of 2.5cm (1in). Using a 7.5cm (3in) circular pastry cutter, cut out the scones and place on the baking sheet. Press the trimmings together, roll out and repeat the process until you have used all the dough.

Brush each scone with a little milk and sprinkle with sugar. Place in the oven on the middle shelf and bake for 12–14 minutes until they have risen and turned a lovely golden-brown colour on top.

Transfer to a wire rack to cool slightly before serving warm with a little butter and jam.

CARROT & CARDAMOM CAKE
WITH CINNAMON CREAM CHEESE FROSTING

Carrot and cardamom are a wonderful combination of flavours. The cake itself is moist enough but for that extra special touch you can add the delicious cinnamon cream cheese frosting. If you want to go all out, you can make mini carrots out of marzipan with a little orange food colouring and angelica root for the stalks.

☛ SERVES 8

Butter, for greasing

275g (10oz) self-raising flour

½ tsp bicarbonate of soda

1 tsp ground cinnamon

1 tsp cardamom pods, split and seeds ground

275g (10oz) caster sugar

4 large free-range eggs

250ml (9fl oz) rapeseed oil

1 tbsp vanilla extract

400g (14oz) carrots, peeled and finely grated

For the frosting

200g (7oz) cream cheese

50g (2oz) softened butter

450g (1lb) icing sugar

1 tsp ground cinnamon

Preheat the oven to 180°C (350°F), Gas Mark 4. Grease two 23cm (9in) springform cake tins with removable bases and line the bases with a circular disc of parchment paper.

In a large bowl, mix together the flour, bicarbonate of soda, cinnamon and cardamom with a wooden spoon.

In a standalone mixer (or in a large bowl, using an electric hand mixer), whisk together the sugar and eggs until pale and fluffy. With the mixer still on, pour the oil into the bowl, in a steady stream, and mix until it is completely incorporated, then mix in the vanilla extract.

Sift the dry ingredients into the batter and fold in with a spatula until just mixed through. Add the finely grated carrot and fold through until completely incorporated. Divide the batter between the two lined cake tins and place in the oven to bake for 30 minutes or until a skewer inserted comes out clean.

Remove the cakes from the oven and set aside to cool on a wire rack. When the tins are cool enough to touch, gently release the cakes and return them to the wire rack, removing the base and parchment paper. Allow to cool completely. If one of the cakes has risen more than the other, simply cut off the excess with a bread knife so that you have a flat surface to work with.

Prepare the frosting by beating the cream cheese, butter, icing sugar and cinnamon until you have a smooth, spreadable mix.

Assemble the cake by spreading one of the layers with half the cream cheese frosting. Place the second layer on top and spread with the remaining frosting. Slice into eight slices and serve. The cake will keep in the fridge for 3–5 days.

FROZEN CHOCOLATE CHIP COOKIES

I'm always on the lookout for a great chocolate-chip cookie recipe, and this one is adapted from a famous *New York Times* recipe, which produces chewy cookies. The dough benefits from resting overnight in the fridge and also freezes extremely well. I've called them 'frozen' chocolate chip cookies because I always make up a large batch and put rolls of the dough in the freezer. If doing this, allow them to thaw slightly before cutting into circles and baking.

 MAKES 12

275g (10oz) soft light brown sugar

225g (8oz) granulated sugar

275g (10oz) butter

2 large free-range eggs

1 tbsp vanilla extract

475g (1lb 10z) plain flour

2 tsp baking powder

300g (11oz) good-quality milk chocolate, roughly chopped into chunks

Sea salt

In a standalone mixer with a paddle beater (or in a large bowl, using an electric hand mixer), beat the sugars and butter until light and pale. Break in the eggs one at a time, mixing between additions and pausing to scrape down the sides with a spatula. Mix in the vanilla extract.

Remove the bowl from the mixer and sift in the flour and baking powder. Mix with a wooden spoon until well incorporated, then mix through the chocolate chunks. Bring the dough together and split into two. Place each half on a sheet of cling film, roll up and form into a thick sausage shape, sealing the ends.

Depending on how many cookies you need (the sausages make six cookies each, or more if you make them smaller), you can place one of the cookie-dough sausages in the freezer for another time and one in the fridge to rest overnight. The frozen dough will last up to 6 months in the freezer. Simply pop it in the fridge, or give it an extremely cautious 30-second blast in the microwave before you plan to use it.

The following day, take the dough out of the fridge, unwrap and slice into six pieces. Place the slices onto a lined baking sheet and sprinkle each cookie with a little sea salt. Preheat the oven to 180°C (350°F), Gas Mark 4.

Pop in the oven to bake for 20 minutes or until they are golden brown on the edges and ever so slightly pale in the centre. Allow to cool slightly before transferring to a wire rack to cool completely.

BANANA & OATMEAL
MUFFINS

I love to make these muffins for breakfasts and brunches; they are quite filling and a nice start to the day. You could add berries, chopped apple or stir through chocolate chips for an extra hit of sweetness.

 ## MAKES 12

125g (4½oz) plain flour

75g (2½oz) wholemeal flour

200g (7oz) rolled oats, plus extra for sprinkling

75g (2½oz) soft light brown sugar

1 tbsp baking powder

1 tsp ground cinnamon

250ml (9fl oz) milk

2 large free-range eggs, separated

3 tbsp rapeseed oil

1 tbsp cold coffee

2 bananas, mashed, plus 1 banana, cut into 12 slices

Preheat the oven to 200°C (400°F), Gas Mark 6. Line a muffin or cupcake tray with 12 paper cases.

In a large bowl, combine the flours, oats, sugar, baking powder and cinnamon.

Measure the milk in a large measuring jug and whisk in the egg yolks, oil, coffee and mashed bananas. In a clean bowl, whisk the egg whites until they form soft peaks.

Make a well in the centre of the dry ingredients and pour in the contents of the jug. Using a spatula, mix together until just combined. Fold through the egg whites, then divide the mixture amongst the paper cases.

Push a slice of banana into the centre of each muffin and sprinkle with oats. Place in the oven to bake for 25 minutes until golden on top.

Remove from the oven and allow to cool slightly before transferring to a wire rack to cool completely. The muffins will keep for 4–5 days in an airtight container or for up to 3 months in resealable bags in the freezer.

BAKED LEMON & POPPY SEED
CHEESECAKE

You can make the base with any type of biscuit you like, but bear in mind that some biscuits will require more or less butter in order for the base to set.

400g (14oz) ginger biscuits
150g (5oz) butter, melted
500g (1lb 2oz) cream cheese
175g (6oz) caster sugar
Grated zest and juice of 1 lemon
3 large free-range eggs
1 tbsp poppy seeds

Preheat the oven to 160°C (325°F), Gas Mark 3. Use a circular disc of parchment paper to line a 20cm (8in) cake tin with a removable base.

Blitz the ginger biscuits in a food processor until you have very fine crumbs. Pour in the butter and give the mixture another blitz until it is the texture of wet sand. Empty the biscuit crumbs into the lined cake tin and press into the base and sides. Place in the fridge to firm up while you prepare the filling.

In a standalone mixer (or in a large bowl, using an electric hand mixer) beat the cream cheese, sugar and lemon zest until smooth. Add the eggs one at a time, making sure to fully incorporate each one before adding the next. Beat in the lemon juice until combined. Using a spatula, fold through the poppy seeds.

Pour the mixture onto the biscuit base – it should come to about 2cm (¾in) below the top of the tin. Tap the tin gently to release any air and smooth the top with the spatula. Place on the middle shelf of the oven and bake for 1 hour until the filling is just set. There should still be a slight wobble in the centre, which will set as it cools.

Turn the oven off and open the door slightly, leaving the cheesecake inside to cool completely, then cover and place in the fridge to chill for at least 2 hours before serving.

ISKEROON IRISH
SODA BREAD

David Hare, who produces my TV show *Kitchen Hero*, passed on this recipe when we stayed with him and his family, Geraldine, Patrick and Mella, during some of the shooting in Caherdaniel, Kerry. The bread is incredibly easy to make.

 **MAKES 1 LOAF**

450g (1lb) wholemeal flour, plus extra for dusting

1 tsp bicarbonate of soda

Generous pinch of salt

Generous pinch of sugar

350ml (12fl oz) buttermilk

Handful of jumbo rolled oats

Irish butter, to serve

Preheat the oven to 230°C (450°F), Gas Mark 8. Combine all the dry ingredients, except for the oats, in a bowl.

Make a well in the middle and pour in the buttermilk. Using a wooden spoon, combine the wet and dry ingredients until you have a sticky mixture.

Use your hands to shape the dough into a ball. Place it on a floured baking tray and sprinkle over the oats. Cook in the oven for 15 minutes, then reduce the temperature to 200°C (400°F), Gas Mark 6 and cook for another 20 minutes until nicely browned on top. The bread is done when you tap it underneath and it sounds hollow.

Remove from the oven and allow to cool before slathering with a good bit of Irish butter and devouring!

IRISH
BARMBRACK

Barmbrack is a traditional Irish fruit cake, which I used to get in my school lunchbox around Halloween every year. Traditionally, a ring is baked into the cake, and there would be great excitement every year as to who would get the slice with the ring in it. I always like to think it was Barmbrack that inspired the writers of *Father Ted* to come up with the episode where Mrs. Doyle bakes a jumper into a cake! This recipe makes a really beautiful, moist loaf, packed with flavour from the mixed spice and dried fruit, which has sat overnight in cold tea and whiskey to soak up all the goodness.

SERVES 4

1 x 375g (13oz) packet of mixed dried fruit

50ml (2fl oz) whiskey

250ml (9fl oz) cold tea

Butter, for greasing

225g (8oz) plain flour

2 tsp baking powder

125g (4½oz) soft light brown sugar

½ tsp mixed spice

1 large egg

A ring, to place inside (optional)

Place the mixed dried fruit in a bowl and pour over the whiskey and cold tea. Allow to soak up the liquid overnight.

Preheat the oven to 170°C (325°F), Gas Mark 3. Grease and line a 900g (2lb) loaf tin.

Combine the flour, baking powder, sugar and mixed spice in a mixing bowl. Make a well and break in the egg, then use a wooden spoon to mix it with the dry ingredients. Add a little bit of the liquid from the mixed fruit and mix it through. You may not need all the liquid, though you are looking for a wet dough.

Stir in the mixed fruit until everything is thoroughly combined. Add the ring, if you like, and stir it through. Spoon the wet dough into the lined loaf tin, place on the middle shelf in the oven and bake for 1 hour.

Remove from the oven and allow to cool slightly before removing from the loaf tin and placing on a wire rack. Cover in cling film and foil and allow to sit for 1–2 days before cutting into it. Serve in slices, spread with a little butter and accompanied by a good cuppa!

SWEDISH GINGERBREAD

This recipe makes perfectly crisp gingerbread biscuits that snap and crumble in the mouth. The smell of them baking in the oven will instantly transport you to Christmas heaven! These quantities make a huge amount of cookies because traditionally the Swedes bake loads of these to give away as presents and to have in the house when people call round during the festive season. There is also enough dough here to use for a gingerbread house. However, the dough does freeze extremely well, so if you don't want to use it all, freeze half of it in cling film for up to 6 months. Ideally, you want to start making this dough a day beforehand so that you have enough time to leave it to develop overnight.

 **MAKES 100 BISCUITS (APPROX)**

150ml (5fl oz) golden syrup
250g (9oz) caster sugar
200g (7oz) butter
150ml (5fl oz) single cream
1 tsp ground ginger
1 tsp ground cinnamon
1 tsp bicarbonate of soda
700g (1½lb) plain flour, plus extra for dusting

Place a large cooking pot over a medium heat and add the golden syrup, sugar and butter. Cook the mixture until the butter has melted and the sugar is completely dissolved.

Take the pot off the heat and stir through the cream and spices. Add the bicarbonate of soda and then the flour, a little at a time, stirring with a wooden spoon until you have mixed it all through. Work the dough together until you have a loose mixture. Cover and leave in a cool place overnight; the next day you should have a thick dough.

When ready to bake, preheat the oven to 180°C (350°F), Gas Mark 4. Line two baking trays with silicone baking mats or dust with flour.

Dust a work surface with flour and roll out the dough to a thickness of about 2mm (¹/₁₆ in), or as thin as you can, because you want the biscuits to rise only slightly so they will be nice and crisp when cool.

Using cutters of your choice (though you can't go wrong with a gingerbread-man shape!), cut out the biscuits and place as many as will fit on the lined or floured baking trays, leaving about 2cm (¾in) between them. If baking the full amount of biscuits, you will have to put them in the oven in batches, so set the rest aside for the moment. Make sure to use up the pastry scraps by pressing them together so that you can roll out the dough again and cut more biscuits.

Bake in the oven for 8–10 minutes or until the biscuits are a rich brown colour at the sides and slightly pale in the middle. Remove from the oven and place on a wire rack to cool. Store the biscuits in a tin or airtight container so that they stay nice and crisp.

AUNTIE ANN'S BANANA BREAD
WITH RICH FUDGE FROSTING

This recipe comes from my auntie Ann, who has spent a lot of time in America over the years and picked up some really great US-inspired recipes. This banana bread is deliciously moist and extremely easy to throw together. The topping is completely optional and, in fact, warm slices of this bread with just a little butter is all you really need!

MAKES 2 LOAVES
900G (2LB)

110g (4oz) butter, plus extra for greasing

190g (6½oz) caster sugar

2 large free-range eggs

240g (8½oz) self-raising flour, sifted

1 tsp bicarbonate of soda

3 large bananas

½ tsp vanilla extract

For the fudge topping

220g (¾oz) soft dark brown sugar

35g butter

75ml (2½fl oz) milk

1 tbsp single cream

Preheat the oven to 180°C (350°F), Gas Mark 4. Grease two 900g (2lb) loaf tins.

Cream the butter and sugar in a large bowl with an electric hand mixer until it is light and pale. Add one egg and a little flour and mix through. Repeat with the other egg, the rest of the flour and the bicarbonate of soda, mixing until everything is combined and smooth.

Peel the bananas and mash with the back of a fork. Add to the bowl with the vanilla extract and mix through. Divide the mixture between the two loaf tins and place on the middle shelf of the oven for approximately 50 minutes. If you need to, you can cover with foil after 25 minutes to stop the bread browning too much on top.

Insert a metal skewer into the centre of each loaf; if it comes out clean, the banana bread is ready. Remove from the tins and place on a wire rack to cool.

For the topping, combine the brown sugar, butter and milk in a saucepan. Place over a medium–high heat and stir continuously until the sugar is dissolved. Then cook without stirring for 10–15 minutes until a teaspoonful of mixture forms a soft ball when it is dropped in cold water.

Put the topping into a small bowl and allow to cool to lukewarm, then beat until it begins to thicken. Add the cream a little at a time and continue beating until you have a spreading consistency. Spread onto the loaves straight away and enjoy a generous slice with a big cup of tea.

MOIST MAPLE APPLE
TEA CAKE

I collect vintage cookbooks and I got the idea for this cake after being given a gift of a big pile of 1950s Swedish cookery books. The recipe that kept coming up was one for apple cake and I knew I had to try it. The smells from this cake wafting around the house are unbelievable and the result is a rich, moist and sticky cake.

☞ SERVES 6–8

110g (4oz) butter, plus extra for greasing

200g (7oz) soft light brown sugar

2 large free-range eggs

210g (7½oz) plain flour, sifted

1 tbsp baking powder

Pinch of salt

1 tsp ground cinnamon

250g (9oz) peeled, cored and diced cooking apple (about 1 apple)

4 tbsp maple syrup

Ice cream, to serve (optional)

Preheat the oven to 180°C (350°F), Gas Mark 4. Grease and line a 20cm (8in) cake tin with a removable base.

With an electric hand mixer, beat the butter and sugar in a large bowl until pale. Add the eggs, one at a time, mixing until they are incorporated. Fold through the flour, baking powder, salt and cinnamon until you have a thick cake batter.

Stir through the apple and pour the batter into the cake tin. The batter will be thick, so use a spatula to spread it across the base of the tin. Bake in the oven for 55 minutes.

Remove from the oven and poke all over with a skewer. Pour over the maple syrup a little bit at a time, allowing the cake to soak it up. Leave to cool and then serve in generous slices as tea cake, or with a little ice cream for dessert.

AUNTIE ERICA'S
IRISH OAT FLAPJACKS

There are certain tastes that instantly transport you back to being a kid. My aunt Erica used to bring us trays of flapjacks when she looked after us and I've loved them ever since. Flapjacks are a great storecupboard recipe that uses ingredients you are bound to have in the house.

 MAKES 10

75g (2½oz) butter, plus extra for greasing

50g (2oz) soft light brown sugar

2 tbsp golden syrup

175g (6oz) rolled oats

Preheat the oven to 180°C (350°F), Gas Mark 4. Grease a shallow 18cm (7in) square baking tin.

Melt the butter with the sugar and syrup in a pan over a low heat, then pour it onto the rolled oats in a large bowl. Mix well, then pour the mixture into the prepared tin and press down well.

Bake in the oven for about 20 minutes, until golden brown. Allow to cool slightly in the tin, then mark into fingers with a sharp knife and loosen round the edges.

When firm, remove from the tin and cool on a wire rack, then break into fingers. These will store well for up to 1 week.

ULTIMATE CHOCOLATE FUDGE CAKE WITH WHITE CHOCOLATE FROSTING

Now, I know ultimate chocolate fudge cakes don't exactly scream 'food for less', but on special occasions the purse strings must be loosened and this particular cake will feed an army – well, maybe a small army! Plus, making your own is cheaper than buying from a posh cake shop, and you'll have ingredients left over to bake more cakes! The beauty of this recipe is that it's simply a case of combining wet and dry ingredients to create a light yet fudgy chocolate cake. Be warned: this makes a GIANT cake, so halve the quantities if you want to reduce the size.

 **MAKES 1 LARGE CAKE**
SERVES 8–12

Butter, for greasing

350g (12oz) self-raising flour

5 tbsp cocoa powder

2 tsp bicarbonate of soda

300g (11oz) caster sugar

4 large free-range eggs, beaten

300ml (10½fl oz) sunflower oil

300ml (10½fl oz) semi-skimmed milk

4 tbsp golden syrup

For the frosting

400g (14oz) good-quality white chocolate

220g (¾oz) butter, at room temperature

450g (1lb) cream cheese

440g (15½oz) icing sugar

Preheat the oven to 180°C (350°F), Gas Mark 4. Grease two 23cm (9in) cake tins with removable bases and line with parchment paper.

Sift the flour, cocoa and bicarbonate of soda into the bowl of a standalone mixer (or use a large bowl and an electric hand mixer). Add the sugar and mix well.

Measure the wet ingredients into a measuring jug. Make a well in the centre of the dry ingredients and pour in the contents of the jug. Beat together with the mixer until you have a smooth mixture.

Spoon the cake batter into the lined tins and bake for 45–50 minutes, or until risen and firm to the touch. Remove from the oven and leave to cool before transferring to a wire rack until completely cool.

To make the frosting, melt the chocolate in a heatproof bowl placed over a saucepan filled with a little water boiling over a low heat. Remove from the heat to cool for about 10 minutes.

Place the butter and cream cheese in a bowl and beat until fluffy and combined. Mix through the melted white chocolate, then gradually sift and beat in the icing sugar until you have a smooth, spreadable mixture.

Slice both cake layers in half horizontally and place one on a cake stand. Spread over a little of the frosting, then repeat with all the layers until the cake is assembled. If you want, you can spread frosting on the outside of the cake too – this will use the full quantity of frosting.(If you choose not to do this, any leftover frosting can be kept in the fridge for 2 weeks, covered directly with cling film, or it can be frozen for up to 6 months.)

BETTY'S
AMBROSIA CAKE

One of my favourite things to do is to talk on the topic of food with my granny. Learning to cook armed only with cookbooks and a passion for art, with eight hungry mouths to feed and very little money, my granny developed some of the most resourceful cooking skills I know. I love that with barely anything in the house she can produce something incredibly elegant, such as soufflés, without thinking twice. This is a light and rather sophisticated cake that relies heavily on storecupboard ingredients and is a perfect example of her skill in being able to produce something incredibly impressive out of everyday items.

☛ SERVES 6

140g (5oz) butter, melted, plus extra for greasing
2 tbsp fine breadcrumbs
2 large free-range eggs
110g (4oz) caster sugar
110g (4oz) plain flour
½ tsp baking powder
100g (3½oz) icing sugar
2 tbsp orange juice
Grated zest of ½ orange
Toasted skinned almonds, to decorate

Preheat the oven to 200°C (400°F), Gas Mark 6 and grease a 20cm (8in) cake tin with a removable base. Sprinkle in the breadcrumbs.

Beat the eggs and sugar in a medium-sized mixing bowl with a whisk until pale and light. Sift the flour into a separate bowl, then make a well in the centre and pour in the melted butter. Using a wooden spoon, mix thoroughly until you have a smooth batter.

Gently fold in the egg and sugar mixture, along with the baking powder, until combined. Pour into the prepared cake tin and bake on the middle shelf of the oven for about 45 minutes. Remove from the oven and allow to cool on a wire rack.

When completely cool, transfer to a cake stand. Whisk together the icing sugar, orange juice and zest and drizzle over the cake. Decorate with the toasted almonds and allow to set before serving in generous slices with coffee or tea.

INDEX

Entries in *italics* indicate photographs.

ACKNOWLEDGEMENTS

The first thank you has to go to my **granny** who I suppose inspired this book in many ways. She was my first port of call on all things frugal cooking and it was her interest in food and cooking which spurred my mom's interest and in turn mine.

To my **mom** and **dad**, **family** and **friends** who are my very best supporters and promoters. The cheque's in the post!

To my **aunt Erica Ryan** for the fantastic food styling and for enduring two long weeks of a massive kitchen invasion while I shot the photographs for this book.

To my agent **Eavan Kenny**, thank you for making everything run as smoothly as it does and even for washing up after the odd cookery demo (not part of the job description!) and to **Faith**, **Lisa** and **Richard** at Lisa Richards agency for the great guidance and advice!

To **Orla Broderick**, who had the tough job of testing the recipes, thanks for the wonderful and detailed meetings about the recipes and everything in between.

We had so much fun shooting the cover for the book and it was all thanks to the great spirit of the whole team involved, **Tom Wilcox** and **Elliott Cole**, **Polly Webb-Wilson**, **Annie Hudson** and **Rachel Wood**, **Annette Field**, **Eliisa Makin**, and of course to the ringleaders, the fab **Kate Gaughran** and **Heike Schuessler** for their enthusiasm! To **Elen Jones**, **Helen Wedgewood**, **Martin Topping**, **Lucy Sykes-Thompson** a big thank you for all the work behind the scenes. Also to the wonderful **Ione Walder** for crossing the 't's and dotting the 'i's!

To the fabulous **Lizzy Gray** at Collins who set the wheels of this book into motion, and for giving me wonderful direction throughout its creation.

To **Brian Walsh** at RTÉ who is always full of support and wise words, thank you! To **David Hare** for his great advice and for patiently listening to all my wild ideas and then turning them into something worth watching! To the most puntastic camera and sound duo in the industry, **Billy** and **Ray**, thanks a mill for the great fun we have filming!

To **Moira T Reilly** from HarperCollins and **Ann Coughlin** and **Pauline Cronin** from TVPR for doing an absolutely superb job at promoting the book and TV series. Three ladies who are definitely a force to be reckoned with!

To **Julie-Anne Hanley** and **Peter Hewitt** from Bosch for arranging the wonderful kitchen appliances featured in the show. I promise to stop telling people I use the plate warmer for drying my undies!

A massive thank you to the **Irish Crafts Council** for arranging the use of plates, bowls, boards, glasses, cake stands from their many highly talented members. **Rosemarie Durr** (pages 44-5, 58-9, 110-11, 190-1, www.rosedurr.com), **Jerpoint Glass** (pages 31, 110-11, 172-3, www.jerpointglass.com), **Lynda Gault** (pages 108-9, www.lyndagaultceramics.ie), **Nicholas Mosse** (pages 94-5, 143-4, 184-5, www.nicholasmosse.com), **Little Hill Design** (pages 180-1, www.littlehilldesign.ie), **Sinead Lough** (pages 38-9, 92-3, 132-3, 136-7, 196-7, www.sineadloughceramics.com), **Karen Morgan** (pages 98-9, 103-4, www.karenmorganceramics.com), **Avoca** (www.avoca.ie)

To **Auntie Ann** for the continual use of plates and fabrics used throughout the shoot.

Historic Interiors for use of their beautiful old tables and various other props which we used during the shoot

Sean Gallagher from Patchworkveg.com who not only fitted some fantastic raised vegetable boxes in my garden but also provided me with some of the great wooden backgrounds you see in the images of this book.

Our local butcher **Ray Collier** from Collier's Butchers in Howth who always has the best cut and gave me lots of detailed information for the frugal cooking guide.

My fishy friend **Martin McLoughlin** from Nicky's Plaice in Howth who is always full of advice on what to buy and for patiently letting me get his good side!

Joe Doherty who runs the fantastic Country Market in Howth for diligently posing for the frugal cooking guide.

Finally to **Sofie**, thanks for the constant support and love, and for keeping me somewhat sane! :)

First published in 2012 by Collins
HarperCollins*Publishers*
77–85 Fulham Palace Road
London W6 8JB

www.harpercollins.co.uk

16 15 14 13 12
9 8 7 6 5 4 3 2 1

A catalogue record for this book is available from the
British Library.

ISBN: 978-0-00-741550-2
Design by Lucy Sykes-Thompson
Props, Sofie Larsson
Food Stylist, Erica Ryan

Printed and bound in Italy by L.E.G.O. SpA

MIX
Paper from
responsible sources
FSC
www.fsc.org
FSC™ C007454

FSC™ is a non-profit international organisation established to promote the
responsible management of the world's forests. Products carrying the FSC
label are independently certified to assure consumers that they come from
forests that are managed to meet the social, economic and ecological needs
of present and future generations, and other controlled sources.

Find out more about HarperCollins and the environment at
www.harpercollins.co.uk/green